BERLITZ®

SRI LANKA
and the Maldives

1992/1993 Edition

By the staff of Berlitz Guides

Copyright © 1991, 1981 by Berlitz Publishing S.A.,
Avenue d'Ouchy 61, 1000 Lausanne 6, Switzerland.

Library of Congress Catalog Card No. 81-67094.

Berlitz Trademark Reg. U.S. Patent Office
and other countries – Marca Registrada.

Printed in Switzerland by Weber S.A., Bienne.

9th Printing
1992 / 1993 Edition

Updated or revised 1991, 1989, 1988, 1986,
1985, 1983, 1982

How to use our guide

- All the practical information, hints and tips that you will need before and during the trip start on page 105.
- For general background, see the sections The Island and the People, p. 6, and A Brief History, p. 13.
- All the sights to see are listed between pages 27 and 78. Our own choice of sights most highly recommended is pinpointed by the Berlitz traveller symbol. A special section on the Maldives with its own practical information summary is to be found between pages 78 and 84.
- Entertainment, nightlife and all other leisure activities are described between pages 85 and 97, while information on restaurants and cuisine is to be found on pages 98 to 104.
- Finally, there is an index at the back of the book, pp. 126–128.

Although we make every effort to ensure the accuracy of all the information in this book, changes occur incessantly. We cannot therefore take responsibility for facts, prices, addresses and circumstances in general that are constantly subject to alteration. Our guides are updated on a regular basis as we reprint, and we are always grateful to readers who let us know of any errors, changes or serious omissions they come across.

Text: Jack Altman
Photography: Claude Huber
Layout: Doris Haldemann
We wish to extend our special thanks to Roland Edirisinghe and Annesley Henricus for their collaboration in the preparation of this guide. We are very grateful to the Ceylon Tourist Board, and especially to H. P. Siriwardsana in Colombo and to Sam. M. Samaradivakara of the Frankfurt office. Sharmali Bamunsingse Andrey and Gunapala also made a considerable contribution to the realization of this project.

4 Cartography: Falk-Verlag, Hamburg.

Contents

Maps

Cover picture: Devil mask from Ambalangoda

The Island and the People

Sri Lanka is not the new name for Ceylon. It's the old one. Retrieved in 1972 from 2,500 years of history, it means, approximately and appropriately, Splendid Land. An island of richly varied landscapes, Sri Lanka combines lush jungle and rolling hill country, brilliant green tea plantations and palm-fringed beaches—the whole embraced by the soothing waters of the Indian Ocean. As a name, Splendid Land seems to do very nicely.

The island, they say, is

shaped like a pear, like a pearl, like a tear dropped from the vast sub-continent of India. The constant association of Sri Lanka with India is inevitable and historically and culturally proper. But it would be wrong to think of the island as nothing more than an extension of its neighbour to the north-west. In the process of wresting itself, first geologically and then politically, from the sub-continent Sri Lanka has developed a distinctive personality.

Peace in the quiet work of batik and the sea and sand of Hikkaduwa.

Sinhala is a language unique to the island and Sinhalese culture a source of enduring pride, with literacy well over 80 per cent. Buddhism flourishes in Sri Lanka—having been supplanted by Hinduism in India—and has by and large been a force for calm in an area of the world so often shaken by violent extremes.

Conflict on the island has been making headlines for several years now. The Tamils, a Hindu minority of Indian origin (about 18 per cent in a population of 15 million), have resorted to violence in their struggle against discrimination by the dominant Sinhalese, frequently with bloody results. There appears to be no solution in sight, as the fires of revolt and its repression continue to disturb the island's one-time tranquillity.

Despite the ethnic tensions, Sri Lanka lacks the giant passions of India—and so, perhaps, much of its excitement, too. It offers a quieter charm.

Sinhalese in Sanskrit signifies "People of the Lion", but this fierce connotation is usually blotted out by their easy-going nature. The Tamils live mostly in the north and east of the island. They are a dour people—hard-working,

dignified, not as accessible as the Sinhalese, but just as unfailingly polite. Other even smaller minorities include the Muslims, descendants of medieval Arab traders, and the Burghers, whose lighter skins and European names derive from 16th- and 17th-century colonization.

Vestiges of Portuguese occupation are rare in terms of monuments or buildings. Portugal's real legacy is the abiding Catholicism of the west coast fishing villages. The Dutch bequeathed a network of canals around Colombo and the sturdy forts that dot the coast from the northern city of Jaffna to the historic southern port town of Galle. But the most insistent colonial ghosts are, of course, the most recent.

British rule from the time of the Napoleonic wars to the end of World War II has left Sri Lankans with a world language, an administrative structure and a series of splendid old colonial residences and clubs, many converted into hotels, court-houses and museums. "Ceylon Breakfast Tea" is served with the same ritual as in the days of empire. Tea

Perhaps not nirvana yet, but a moment of peace for this Buddhist monk.

8

is still an important export, along with rubber and coconut products. Sri Lanka's British heritage has naturally enough undergone some subtle changes. The English language, resisted for many years in a quest for Sinhalese identity, is a picturesque mixture of 1920s idiom and modern jargon.

One British legacy in bad need of a more than subtle change is the bus system. Rickety old vehicles, beneath their grime most probably red in colour, thunder along like berserk monsters out of hell, spewing forth smoke and occasionally disgorging passengers at "Motor Bus Halting Places". Everybody curses them, but they have absolute priority on the road. You don't pick a fight with a Sri Lankan bus. It is typical of the nation's good humour that the totally dreadful bus system is generally regarded with affection. Miraculously it does get people to their destinations.

Driving on the island is a challenging adventure. Buses may take pride of place in the traffic chamber of horrors, but they are closely followed by the mad lorries, carefree taxis and completely oblivious bicycles. Motorists run an obstacle race around the ever-present

cows, occasional elephants, the chickens, goats and dogs—many of the latter all too significantly three-legged—who wander along the roads or just fall asleep in the middle. An important motto of Sri Lanka is "Live and let live"—if you can.

For life by and large is not too difficult. People look very comfortable in their sarongs and saris, national costumes that still hold their own against Western dress. Sri Lanka lies

10

Tea in the hills of Nuwara Eliya is a legacy of the British empire.

close to the equator, so the year is divided into dry and rainy seasons rather than spring, summer, autumn and winter. And you usually have a choice. When the monsoon prevails on the north-east side of the island from November to February, it's sunny in the south-west. When the south-west coast has its monsoon from May to September, it's dry on the opposite side. And if you want to get away from the heat, you can always fol-low the example of the British colonials and head for the hill country around Nuwara Eliya. You could be in Scotland. There's even a golf course.

The commercial centre, Colombo, is always hot and sticky. But out on the beaches near the metropolis, it's easy to beat the heat. In the south-west, the beaches stretch from **11**

Negombo to Galle and on to Tangalla, while the east coast beaches, less crowded but no less attractive, go from Nilaveli, past the lovely bay of Trincomalee to Kalkudah.

But the island offers more than a lazy holiday on the beach. Ancient cities like Anuradhapura and Polonnaruwa provide fascinating glimpses of Sri Lanka's proud past, with their crumbling temples and granite Buddhas impervious to the onslaught of time and the elements. There's the old royal capital of Kandy and Adam's Peak, the mountain top where Adam, Buddha or the Hindu god Shiva (depending on your religion) is said to have stepped. And the noblest creatures of all: the elephants. Some 2,000 of them roam wild, mostly in nature reserves like Yala and Wilpattu. Another 500 labour on building sites and in timberland.

If Sri Lanka sounds almost too good to be true, remember that it's the island immortalized in the fairy tale *The Three Princes of Serendip.* The name Serendip gave rise to the lovely word "serendipity" —the gift of finding valuable or agreeable things without looking for them. And Sri Lanka offers this gift to every tourist.

Sri Lanka in a Nutshell

Geography Sri Lanka is an island in the Indian Ocean, with an area of 25,332 square miles. The cool central region has hills and mountains, while the humid coastal belt is flat. There are two monsoon seasons: May to September in the south-west, November to February in the north-east. The capital is Sri Jayawardenapura, founded in 1982.

Population Estimated at over 15 million. Colombo, the commercial centre and largest city, counts around 700,000 inhabitants. Sri Lanka's principal ethnic groups are Sinhalese. Tamils, Muslims and Burghers.

Religion Buddhism enjoys state support. There are also Hindu, Muslim and Christian minorities.

Industry Plywood, paper, glassware, ceramics. Chief crops include rice, copra, rubber and tea. Among the country's exports are tea, fish, spices, minerals and precious stones.

Languages Sinhala, Tamil, English.

Currency Sri Lanka Rupee (Re 1 = 100 cents).

A Brief History

The earliest settlers of Sri Lanka were the Veddahs (Sinhalese for "hunters"), a dark, nomadic people of slight, almost pygmy stature. They belonged to the same racial group as the Australian aborigines and the hill tribes of southern India. Sinhalese legend rather maliciously relates them to the Yakkhas, demons conquered by the forefather of the Sinhalese, the Indian prince Vijaya.

Early Sri Lankan history comes to us from chronicles compiled by Buddhist monks in the 5th century A.D. The *Mahavamsa*, as the earliest is known, merges legend and fact in a deeper truth to account for the spiritual and political shaping of the nation. Typically, Prince Vijaya is said to have arrived near modern Puttalam on the west coast in 483 B.C., which just happens to be the date of Buddha's death and achievement of nirvana.

Vijaya, of Bengali ancestry, had been banished from India by his father because of his violent, rebellious behaviour. (Both Oedipus and Buddha figure prominently in Sri Lanka's history.) He brought 700 followers with him, conquered the resident "demons" and took a "demon-princess" as wife. But, says the *Mahavamsa*, Vijaya was ever mindful of the dignity necessary to founding a nation. He therefore felt obliged to reject his wife and their two offspring—sorrowfully, because a Sinhalese prince is a good father and husband—in favour of a more appropriate Indian princess from the Madurai court.

Archaeology confirms the existence of a 5th century B.C. settlement on the west coast. Tamils probably landed on the east coast near modern Trincomalee, installing themselves inland along the Mahaweli River. A third colony was established at Ruhuna, in the south.

Arrival of Buddhism

The Vijaya capital of Anuradhapura took shape during the 3rd century B.C., and the north-central plains of the island were settled. Government followed the authoritarian Brahmanic pattern of north-east India, but the unifying force of the Sinhalese kingdom was Buddhism.

The Indian emperor Asoka (269–232 B.C.), a devout Buddhist, dispatched his son Mahinda to Sri Lanka as a missionary. It is said that Prince Mahinda flew through **13**

the air, landing on top of Mihintale, a hill that overlooks Anuradhapura. There he intercepted King Tissa, who was out hunting elk, and preached the message of Buddha. Tissa saw the light and let Mahinda and his fellow missionaries set up the Mahavihara monastery; its Buddhist *sangha* (community of monks) made many converts.

No doubt Buddhism had preceded Mahinda's mission. In fact, Buddha himself is said to have visited Sri Lanka three times over 200 years earlier. But King Tissa's conversion provided Buddhism with the impetus it needed to become the established Sinhalese religion and the focus of a strong and positive nationalism.

Tissa and his successors set about consolidating their position. They put the kingdom's agriculture on a sound footing with the construction of an elaborate system of irrigation tanks. The first of them, Tissawewa, can still be seen at Anuradhapura. On an island with rivers but no lakes, these reservoirs were vital for the

This temple at Kelaniya houses a religion of serene contemplation.

Buddhism

Buddhism in Sri Lanka derives from the earliest and purest ethical form, the *Theravada* ("Doctrine of the Elders"). Buddha, Sanskrit for Enlightened One, was born Siddhartha Gautama. He was an Indian prince believed to have lived from around 563 to 483 B.C.

Buddha rejected the spiritual and social supremacy of the priestly Brahmans and their emphasis on sacrifice. He turned from metaphysical to purely ethical values, concerning himself with human suffering and how it might be overcome. Meditating seven weeks under a bo-tree (sacred fig), he realized the need to abandon desire, personal ambition and selfishness.

The path beyond sorrow and suffering lay in a "middle way" between austerity and sensuality. It was an eightfold path of right belief, right resolve, right speech, right conduct, right occupation, right effort, right contemplation and right meditation. The end was nirvana, total blissful detachment, a state it might take many reincarnations to achieve.

A cutting from the bo-tree under which Buddha achieved enlightenment was brought to Sri Lanka from India 2,200 years ago.

15

growing of rice. But the Sinhalese kingdom was far from impregnable. Politically, Sri Lanka was still regarded as an integral part of India, and there was a constant flow of contacts, peaceful and warlike.

Several Tamil rulers conquered the Sinhalese, the most notable being Elara in the 2nd century B.C. In an epic struggle, he was in turn overthrown by the first hero-king of Sinhalese nationalism, Dutugemenu (161–137 B.C.). Sinhalese tradition regards Dutugemenu as a reincarnated Buddhist novice. His spirit is said to have penetrated the womb of his mother, who had been sterile for many years. As a young man, Dutugemenu broke with his father over the latter's reluctance to fight the Tamils. Dutugemenu waged a victorious holy war when he succeeded to the throne, but the gains he made were frittered away by less powerful successors. Invasions from southern India over the next 1,000 years involved Sri Lanka in a perpetual series of dynastic power struggles.

King Mahasena (A.D. 276–303) greatly refined and expanded the vital irrigation system. His most notable achievement was the Minneriya Tank, fed by an intricate network of canals near Giritale. But Mahasena also championed a variety of Buddhist heresies which splintered Sinhalese unity. The oedipal penchant of the Sinhalese royal family was carried to its ultimate conclusion by Kasyapa, who killed his father in 477. Awestruck by what he'd done, he moved his capital to Sigiriya, a fantastic fortress high atop a granite mountain, where he hid out for 18 years (see p. 56).

The Polonnaruwa Period

The constant threat of invasion from India was finally broken in 1070. Vijayabahu drove out the south Indian Cholas and established a new capital at Polonnaruwa, further away from the Indian line of advance. Now there would be more time to prepare a defence against future raids. The new site would also be easier to protect from counter-attacks, since it controlled the route to the south-east region of Ruhuna, where rebels often fled to regroup.

The kingdom experienced its greatest prosperity under Parakramabahu (1153–86), who turned Polonnaruwa into one of Asia's most splendid cities. He ordered construction of the Parakrama Samudra, a water tank vast enough to irrigate 18,000 acres of farmland. Parakramabahu even felt feisty enough to launch a few raids of his own on Burma and south Indian Pandya, impressive but without lasting success.

The Polonnaruwa kings liked to adopt formidable titles such as *deva* (god) or *boddhisattva* (Buddha-to-be). The Buddhist hierarchy indulged this little whim in exchange for a healthy share in state revenues from grain taxes, water dues and the export of surplus grain. During this golden era, Arab merchants developed a profitable trade in rice, ivory, pearls, gems, cinnamon and pepper.

In 1292, Marco Polo passed through Sri Lanka on his way back to Venice from China. He was enraptured by the island's rubies and bemused by the drinking of coconut-palm toddy ("wine drawn from the trees"). But he also remarked on the fact that "the people are averse to a military life". Marco Polo had observed just one sign of the general decline that took place after the halcyon days of Parakramabahu. Indian incursions had resumed. Polonnaruwa fell in 1215 and internecine struggles moved the capital from one place to another—Dambade-niya, Kurunegala, Yapahuva —each more inaccessible than the last. The system of irrigation tanks, once a symbol of the kingdom's strength, crumbled from neglect and deliberate sabotage. By 1500, the island was to be easy pickings for the Portuguese.

The Portuguese Move In

The Portuguese prospected the Indian Ocean area for gold and precious gems, but principally spices. The latter was much prized in the West to disguise the taste of spoiled meats during the era before refrigeration. In November 1505, a fleet of Portuguese caravelles under the command of Lourenço de Almeida was blown into Colombo harbour. The sailors were cordially received by King Vira Parakrambahu, ruler of the kingdom of Kotte in the southwest, and Almeida promptly negotiated a trading station at Colombo.

The Portuguese established a firm footing in Sri Lanka by offering military protection to the kings of Kotte in exchange for trading privileges and an annual tribute of precious cinnamon. Except for a coarse variety found in southern India, the spice was unique to Sri Lanka. To protect the groves **17**

of cinnamon trees from marauders, the Portuguese built a fort at Negombo in 1518.

In 1557 King Dharmapala, educated by Franciscan friars, took the name Don Juan and converted to Christianity. This act outraged the rival kingdoms of Jaffna, Kandy and Sitawake and united warring factions against the Portuguese and their satrap. A rebellion was led by Mayadunne, ruler of Sitawake, and his son Rajasinha. They successfully took control of large areas of the interior. The Portuguese, with their invincible sea power, were content to command the coastal areas and keep an eye on the lucrative cinnamon groves. The coast was also strategic to the consolidation of Portuguese control over the Indian Ocean.

Resistance to Portuguese rule in the interior weakened with the death of Rajasinha in 1593. He had occupied Kandy, a kingdom in the central highlands, since 1580. The Portuguese made several attempts to install their own man on the Kandyan throne, to no avail. In 1594, they proposed a baptized Sinhalese noblewoman, Doña Caterina, as queen. She was brought to Kandy under heavy protection of the Portuguese army, but King Vimala

Chilli spices provided money for the Portuguese gables in Negombo.

Dharma Surya claimed her for himself. He took to the hills and waged guerrilla warfare against the Portuguese.

The northern kingdom of Jaffna held out for 20 years more, and pockets of resistance flared up sporadically along the east coast. Meanwhile, Portuguese commanders pursued private interests, lining their pockets with the quick profits to be made from spices, ivory and betel nuts.

In 1597, Portugal took formal control of Sri Lanka, bequeathed to her in the last will and testament of Don Juan Dharmapala. The island formed part of Portugal's Estado de India and was administered by a captain-general answerable to the viceroy at Goa. The Sinhalese aristocracy learned the Portuguese language and adopted Portuguese **19** surnames. Even today, the telephone books are full of Fernandos and da Silvas. Sri Lanka's guava trees and chilli plants, among other exotic species, were transplanted from Portugal's eastern and South American possessions.

But colonization was neither concerted nor constructive. Extensive Roman Catholic missionary work was undermined by the systematic sacking and destruction of Buddhist and Hindu temples and shrines. One of the most repugnant acts was the public burning of the Sacred Tooth, a revered relic of the Buddha (see p. 67).

Kandy and the Dutch
In the climate of oppression, Sri Lanka was ripe for full-scale rebellion. The ideal focus was the kingdom of Kandy, almost impregnable from attack. But King Vimala Dharma Surya knew total victory would never be his unless he could match Portugal's supremacy at sea. So he looked to the Dutch for help.

Expelling the Portuguese was a long-drawn-out affair of more than 50 years. The massive Portuguese vessels were designed for transporting booty, rather than for military manoeuvrability. They were no match for the smaller,

faster Dutch ships. Portuguese strongholds were attacked at Colombo, Galle, Negombo, Trincomalee and Batticaloa, with the defenders often caught in a pincer assault of Kandyan land forces and Dutch naval vessels.

While the Dutch were battling away at sea, their merchants claimed trade concessions in compensation. It soon became clear that the Dutch intended to replace the Portuguese as European rulers of Sri Lanka. This time, King Rajasinha II thought he could negotiate a better deal for Kandy. But the complexities of dealing with Europeans quickly became apparent. In 1640, the Dutch suddenly made a truce with the Portuguese because of a treaty signed in Europe between the Netherlands and the Spanish empire, of which Portugal was a part. For the time being, the Dutch and the Portuguese carved up Sri Lanka between them.

Rajasinha II did not appreciate the subtleties of European diplomacy and declared a plague on both their houses. He devastated Dutch-occupied territory and in 1649 forced the Dutch to consent to hand back some of the land. However, the fine print made the agreement valid only if the

Dutch were paid for fighting the Portuguese.

When the truce between the Netherlands and Portugal expired in 1652, the two countries went back to fighting each other in earnest. Rajasinha II's Kandyan army drove the Portuguese from the interior all the way back to the coastal strip. He was about to take Colombo when the Dutch asked him to hold off for a while. Their fleet arrived and laid siege for nine months, forcing the Portuguese to surrender in 1656. The Dutch took over and shut out the Kandyans. Miffed, Rajasinha II destroyed the lands around Colombo and went back to his mountains.

The last of the Portuguese were expelled from the northern towns of Mannar and Jaffna by June 1658, and the Dutch East India Company set up shop. A Sinhalese proverb sums up the Sri Lankans' attitude: "We gave pepper and in exchange got ginger."

Masters of the new school of capitalism, the merchants of the Netherlands offered a semblance of tough commercial integrity grafted onto traditional colonial duplicity. They encouraged expansion of rice growing and the cultivation of cash crops like sugar, tobacco and coffee through land grants and tax concessions. The Tamils of Jaffna developed cotton weaving and dyeing. This benefited the Sri Lankans, but it also strengthened Dutch control of the island, since the chiefs who profited were less loyal to the still rebellious kings of Kandy. The Dutch professed to offer Sri Lankans the opportunity to make money from exports to neighbouring countries, but in reality, the amount that could be earned was sharply limited by Dutch controls and restrictions. Ultimately, the most substantial profits were made by smuggling, which Dutch officials permitted—with a rake-off for themselves.

Trying to impose some form of European order on Sri Lankan justice, the new rulers of the island set about codifying Tamil and Muslim law. But they found the Sinhalese legal system too complex, so they just replaced it with Roman-Dutch law. The cruelties of Portuguese colonialism were arbitrary; the Dutch variety was codified.

Calvinism replaced Catholicism. Catholic priests were banished, their churches converted to the Reformed faith. A printing press was set up in 1737 to publish Protestant **21** literature in Sinhalese and Tamil, but it made little impact: Christianity was Christianity, colonialism was colonialism.

The British Take Control

At the end of the 18th century, Sri Lanka's fortunes were again decided thousands of miles away. The Netherlands came under French control and Britain, at war with France, considered Sri Lanka to be fair game. The Dutch put up only half-hearted resistance when the British East India Company came on the scene in 1796. Thinking their takeover might be only temporary, the British administered Sri Lankan affairs from Madras until 1802. But by then it was clear that the island's strategic importance was considerable enough to warrant making it a Crown Colony, a status confirmed by the Treaty of Amiens. The British duly informed the king of Kandy, vowing to honour Kandyan independence.

However, the existence of an autonomous state in the central highlands hindered trade and communications across the island. The British whittled away Kandy's sovereignty by the time-honoured practice of divide-and-rule, pitting discontented aristocrats against their king. And they lulled the Kandyans into a false sense of security by ceremoniously restoring the Sacred Tooth to the shrine of the Dalada Maligawa in 1815.

One British resident of the island, Sir John O'Dwyer, wrote, "We have this day obtained the surest proof of the confidence of the Kandyan nation and their acquiescence in the dominion of the British Government." When the Kandyans at last rebelled, the British took it as a final pretext for asserting complete control over the kingdom, confiscating the Tooth to break the back of the revolt. Kandy was integrated into the rest of the colony and the work of empire went forward.

Roads were built and Christian missionaries expanded the education system. With the opening of the Suez Canal in 1869, the new harbour of Colombo became one of the most important ports in the Indian Ocean. Coffee, farmed by Tamil coolie labour from southern India, grew in importance from 1830 until leaf disease destroyed the crop in 1870. Tea picked up the slack in the 1880s, engulfing the hill country and much of the surrounding lowlands. Coconuts were cultivated on plantations for their lucrative oil and fibre. But the most spectacular success story was rubber, a key contributor to Britain's 19th century prosperity.

Colonialism in its evolution from the Portuguese via the Dutch to the British grew ever more efficient and enterprising, but no less inhuman. A British tea planter wrote in 1900 of the workers: "It is obvious that they do not enjoy the luxury of much space;

Coconut fibre is used to make all kinds of mats, baskets and ropes.

Wicked Wickham

Henry Wickham, rogue capitalist and confidence trickster, travelled to Brazil in 1876. He chartered an ocean liner, the *Amazonas*, and loaded it with 10,000 seeds of *Hevea brasiliensis*, the rubber tree. The seeds had been gathered by an Indian labour force and brought to the confluence of the Amazon and Tapajos rivers.

Wickham bluffed clearance from the Brazilian authorities for his shipload of "exceedingly delicate botanical specimens specially designated for delivery to Her Britannic Majesty's own Royal Gardens of Kew". The only true part of his story was the destination, Kew. There, the orchid houses had been cleared for planting the seeds of the rubber trees, which were later transferred to Sri Lanka and several other British colonies as the foundation of Asia's rubber industry.

but their ideas of comfort are not ours and they are better pleased to lie huddled together upon mud floors in these tiny hovels than to occupy superior apartments."

A reaction from Sri Lankans was inevitable. Buddhism and Hinduism experienced a great revival in the 19th century.

Street festivities pay tribute to the president and local minister.

Schools were established along Western lines, but without the Christian bias of colonial institutions. This nurtured a new political consciousness and led to calls for constitutional reforms that would give Sinhalese and Tamils their own elected officials. By 1910, "educated Ceylonese" could elect members to the Legislative Council, but the majority were still nominated by the British.

A civil disturbance occurred in 1915 and Sinhalese leaders were arrested. But the nationalist movement continued to grow. A Ceylon National Congress uniting Sinhalese and Tamil organizations achieved a greater measure of electoral representation by 1924, but their unity was short-lived. The Sinhalese opposed measures that would have given the Tamils more of a say in government. But the jockeying for governmental positions was little more than an academic exercise until the sun set on the British empire. On February 4, 1948, the colony achieved full independence as a dominion within the British Commonwealth.

Independent Sri Lanka

The country's first prime minister was D.S. Senanayake of the United National Party (U.N.P.) The English education of party leaders gave a conservative flavour to their nationalism. They advocated parliamentary democracy and gradual economic progress through free enterprise. But new leaders, more representative of the mass of Sri Lankans, arose to push for traditional values of religion, language and culture. The U.N.P. was derided for its nepotism as the "Uncle-Nephew Party", and in 1956, S.W.R.D. Bandaranaike led the Sri Lanka Freedom Party into office.

He developed the economy along more socialist lines, and a new wave of nationalism pushed "Sinhalese Only" laws through Parliament to make Sinhala the country's sole official language. State support was extended to Buddhism, as in the days of King Tissa. **25**

Inevitably, the Tamils were alienated. They went into bitter opposition, as did the small but influential Christian minority. May 1958 saw four days of racial violence between Sinhalese and Tamils. Bandaranaike's authoritarian government, no less nepotistic than the U.N.P., also antagonized various Sinhalese factions, and in September 1959, the prime minister was assassinated by a Buddhist monk.

Mrs. Sirimavo Bandaranaike succeeded her husband in 1960, becoming the first woman in the world to serve as prime minister. She continued her husband's socialist policies and nationalized the private schools that had been run by Christian missions. But unemployment, inflation and a shortage of consumer goods forced nationalist preoccupations into the background in 1965 and the U.N.P. returned to power under Dudley Senanayake. Five years later, Mrs. Bandaranaike returned to government and in 1972, the country became a republic, retrieving Sri Lanka as its official name. In 1978, Junius Richard Jayewardene became president under a constitution modelled after that of the Fifth Republic of France. He has had to deal with escalating, if sporadic, outbreaks of violence in Tamil areas—as the juggling of Sri Lanka's ethnic, cultural and religious diversity continues.

Old colonial buildings dominate the Fort, Colombo's city centre.

26

Where to Go*

There's more to Sri Lanka than sandy beaches with palm trees. Even if the main focus of your holiday is the south-west coast with its tourist resorts, you should spend some time exploring the rest of the island.

Once you've seen the city of Colombo, head for the east coast. It's sensible to break the journey from Colombo to Trincomalee at Habarane,

about two-thirds of the way. From here, you can take in the east coast in comfortable stages, going one day to Nilaveli and Trincomalee and then, separately, to Kalkudah, Passekudah and Batticaloa.

This way you'll by-pass the numerous ferry stops on the east coast road, though many insist that the leisurely coastal route is a must for scenic beauty. By using Habarane as your base, you'll be within easy reach of the Ancient Cities region. You can also go over to Kandy and up into the hill country relatively quickly.

Make the trip from Colombo in the morning, as the stretch between Galewela and Habarane is roamed by wild elephants after dark. They're very picturesque, but they don't carry headlights and they won't like yours.

A grand, but slightly dilapidated archway outside the Pettah market.

Colombo

Noisy, frenetic, a little crazy, the city, by its very contrast with the rest of the island, has its own comment to make on Sri Lanka. Some 700,000 people are packed into town, representing every ethnic group in the country—Buddhist Sinhalese, Hindu Tamil, Muslim Arab, Christian Burgher. They're rushing around trying to cope with the demands of a modern metropolis, its traffic, communications problems and constant demolition and reconstruction. But somehow they seem to sense that this intense urban existence is not to be taken too seriously. Breakdowns, traffic jams and electrical blackouts are received with a shrug and a smile. Life goes on. Disconcerted newcomers are constantly reassured with the all-purpose tranquillizing phrase: "No problem". A day or two will get you used to it—and a day or two will do amply to see Colombo's sights.

Central Colombo

It's a good idea to make your walking tour in the early morning or late afternoon, when the heat is manageable. Begin with the **Fort** district.

The Portuguese and Dutch fortifications have long since disappeared, but the name has remained for the city's business centre, with department stores, book shops, main post office, airline offices and some of the big hotels.

A good starting point is the clock tower at the junction of Janadhipathi Mawatha and Chatham Street, a former lighthouse surprisingly far inland from the harbour it was meant to serve. As you go north along Janadhipathi Mawatha towards the harbour, you'll see the immaculate white President's House, still known to some incorrigible traditionalists as Queen's House. Swing into Church Street and you come to the now disused Passenger Harbour Terminal. In colonial times, travellers used to arrive tired and dusty, grateful to stumble across the street into the Grand Oriental Hotel (now the Taprobane) for a restorative gin and tonic. One of the pleasures of Sri Lanka is these old colonial hotels whose faded elegance offers a last glimpse of a time more splendid in the remembering than, as the present owners might insist, in the living of it. Apart from the aura of empire, the Taprobane's Harbour Room

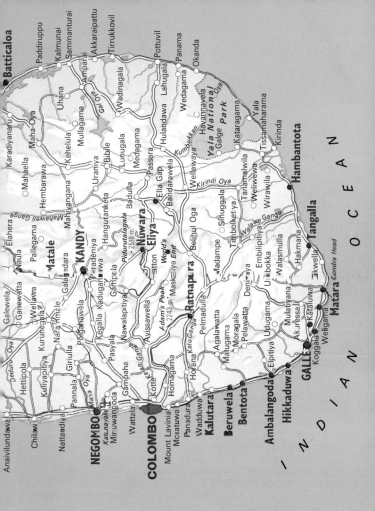

SRI LANKA

Galle Face Green becomes a little brown in the dry season but it's still good for some kite-flying.

restaurant affords an excellent view of ships unloading electrical equipment in exchange for exotic foods.

You might try to wangle your way into the port area (by not dressing too much like a "tourist"). Besides the perverse pleasure of watching others work while you're on holiday, the harbour gives an exciting sense of Colombo's importance as a major Asian port.

Now brace yourself for the **Pettah,** immediately to the east, Colombo's teeming, raucous, pungent bazaar district. A former Dutch residential suburb, the Pettah takes its name from a Tamil word meaning "outside the Fort". Nobody would claim it's beautiful, but your eyes, ears and nose will have missed something if they don't take in this riot of fruit, vegetables, meat, fish, gems, gold and silver treasure, brass and tin junk—all glistening in the sun. As you walk through, most likely in a daze, you may want to stop off to meditate in the striking red-and-white striped Jami-

Ul-Alfar Jumma Mosque at the corner of Bankshall and Second Cross streets. Northeast of the Pettah is the city's oldest church, the 18th-century Dutch Reformed Church of Wolfendahl—the name of a district the Dutch thought was infested by wolves.

South of the Fort area lies spacious **Galle Face Green,** a seafront expanse of lawns that was once the scene of British military manoeuvres. Now it's graced by cricket games and

kite flyers taking advantage of the ocean breezes. The National State Assembly stands at the northern end, together with bronze statues of the political heroes of Sri Lanka's independence movement. At the southern end is Galle Face Hotel, another grand imperial relic with verandahs overlooking the Indian Ocean. A few old retainers still remember watching the sun set on this part of the British empire in 1948.

Colombo Sights

Cinnamon Gardens—commonly known by its prosaic postal address, Colombo 7—is the city's most fashionable neighbourhood. Here, to the south of the city centre, ministers, diplomats and wealthy businessmen live in the gracious old colonial homes of Horton Place, Barnes Place and other noble streets. As you drive around the neighbourhood, you won't see many of the cinnamon trees that gave **33**

the area its name. They were cultivated by the Portuguese and Dutch, who grew rich in the spice trade. But there are well-kept gardens filled with beautiful flowers—anthuriums, roses, bougainvillea, orchids.

The **National Museum,** south of Vihara Maha Devi Park, offers an excellent introduction to the history and culture of Sri Lanka. There are fine examples of Buddhist sculpture and medieval Hindu bronzes, more decorative and sensual than Buddhist artwork. Sinhalese manuscripts from A.D. 957 have the precepts of Buddhist discipline written on panels that look like tiny Venetian blinds. The splendour of old Kandy can be seen in the throne of its last kings and the crown, sceptre and ceremonial sword of King Rajasinha, confiscated by the British in 1815 and returned in 1934. Significantly, the Portuguese and Dutch exhibits comprise iron and copper cannon, many of them with nicely wrought coats of arms. From modern times there is an amusing display of foreign gifts to the head of state: a set of Russian dolls and a model anti-aircraft gun from the Soviet Union, a model space shuttle from the United States, and a war monument from Vietnam showing victorious Vietnamese soldiers dragging away a burned-out piece of a U.S. B-52 bomber with a bullock.

After familiarizing yourself with Sri Lankan culture at the museum, you can get an overview of the island's fauna at the **Dehiwela Zoo,** set in a pleasant park. Take advantage of what may be your only opportunity to glimpse a Sri Lankan leopard while you're on the island. There are several in the national parks (see p. 76), but the chances of seeing one in the wild are slight. This lovely beast is 6 feet long and weighs 100 pounds or more. Among other species on show are monster iguanas, monkeys galore, giant tortoises and elephants (rides all afternoon; circus parade at 5.15 p.m.). The most attractive area of all is the butterfly park, where the island's loveliest species fly free. The Sri Lankans themselves take particular delight in some exotic birds known as swans, from Lake Geneva.

You really can get away from it all on the coast south of Colombo and then read yourself to sleep.

South-west Coast

Swept down from the Persian Gulf by the trade winds, boats from Arabia couldn't help but hit the south-west coast of Sri Lanka. Soon Arab merchants dealing in ivory, spices and precious gems set up trading posts in ports from Negombo to Galle, Matara and Hambantota. Today jumbo jets from London, Frankfurt and Zurich take the same route, flying across the Indian Ocean from Abu Dhabi and Muscat to bring people in search of sea, sand and a precious sun-tan.

The fine beaches and their

sleepy hotels start just north of **Negombo**, a town that derives great charm from its lagoon and fishermen, a much more mellow lot than their Atlantic or Mediterranean counterparts. At dawn—in Sri Lanka you'll very often find yourself awake at dawn—you can watch the prawn boats leave the lagoon to trawl for the justly famous shellfish that gather where the waters of the Maha Oya flow into the sea. If you miss their picturesque departure, you can at least watch the boats return around 10 a.m.—outrigger canoes and Indian-style catamarans, sail-driven log rafts called *katta-maram* in Tamil.

Deep-sea fishing begins well before dawn, but you can attend the auction of the catch—including seir-fish (like mackerel), herring, mullet, pomfret and shark—early in the morning or around 5 p.m. Go to the *lellama* (auction site) near the fort on the north end of the lagoon. The deep-sea fishermen use bigger, motor-driven boats with whaler sterns. They're built at a dozen shipyards, which are well worth visiting. Whole families of 14 or more men and boys—grandfathers, fathers and sons —work away in an atmosphere of cheerful diligence.

The fishermen of Negombo are mostly Catholics, descended from converts of the Portuguese period, when Negombo was a centre of the cinnamon trade. The town's churches far outnumber its temples and mosques. In fact, Negombo is known as "Little Rome".

The resort favoured by Co-

Bringing in the catch at Bentota is a job for all the villagers.

36

lombo's residents and people visiting the town on business is MOUNT LAVINIA. But for a longer stay, you're better off going further down the coast. Along the way, you'll pass through KALUTARA, a centre for the manufacture of coconut by-products, such as mats from the fibre and baskets from the fronds. This is the place to sample the delicious purple mangosteen fruit, completely and startlingly different from the mango (see p. 99).

A large Buddhist shrine stands beside the Kalu Ganga (river). It has a special importance for travellers, and if your driver is a devout believer, you may find him making a two-handed obeisance to the shrine as he passes. Rather than take his hands from the steering-wheel on this treacherous coast road, he can stop the car and put a votive offering in a box beneath the sacred bo-tree.

As you approach Beruwela, you pass an Anglican church

with a polychrome statue of St. George. His face has uncannily Buddha-like features, giving him a much less fierce look than usual, almost as if he regretted having to kill the dragon. **Beruwela** and **Bentota** are neighbouring resorts that merge into each other, like Brighton and Hove. They offer all the sybaritic, soporific pleasures of a sea too blue and a sand too white for a postcard manufacturer to dare pass off as real. But real they are. The lively Alutgama fish market will wake you up if you're hell-bent on some activity.

About 15 miles further south is **Ambalangoda,** capital of the island's celebrated devil-mask industry (see p. 94). Nearby, the Madampe Lagoon offers a beautiful setting of cinnamon trees, coconut palms and rice paddies, perfect for a peaceful picnic.

If Beruwela and Bentota cater more to the family trade, **Hikkaduwa** is the target for singles, swingers and would-bes—one of the few places in Sri Lanka where topless bathing is unofficially tolerated (see p. 111). The beaches are again

Washing in the lagoon is often a pretty sight. The palm trees show you which way the wind's blowing.

superb, and underwater there's an easily accessible and very attractive coral sanctuary, complete with turtles and colourful tropical fish.

Needing no major construction or land-fill to enhance the topography of its natural harbour, **Galle** preceded Colombo as Sri Lanka's first major port. From the early Middle Ages, the Arabs made it an important centre for the ivory and gem trade. The name itself is a source of controversy. It is said that the Portuguese heard the crow of a cock *(galla)* on approaching the harbour for the first time in 1505. But there's also a Sinhalese word, *gala*, meaning rock, the granite rock that forms the harbour's jetty. The Dutch compromised and put a cock crowing on a rocky perch in their coat of arms on the city's ramparts.

Today the town has lost almost all trace of its Portuguese past, but it illustrates splendidly the solidity of the Dutch

presence in Sri Lanka. The massive ramparts of the **Dutch fort** make a fine hour's walk at sunrise or sunset. You can encircle almost the whole fort area, covering 90 acres, on top of walls dating from the 1660s. The most formidable section, known as the Sea Bastion, closed off the neck of land that separates the sea from the harbour. Where the Portuguese had erected a single moated wall, the Dutch constructed a double defence line with three vantage points to repel attackers—the Star, Moon and Sun bastions. Walking south from the Sun Bastion, you cross the Old Gate with a British coat of arms on the outside and the Dutch East India Company's, dated 1669, on the inside; the initials "V.O.C." stand for Vereenigde Oost-Indische Compagnie. The Zwart (Black) Bastion at the northeast tip of the ramparts, the one remaining Portuguese structure, dates back to 1580.

Inside the walls many sturdy old Dutch buildings still stand. Walker and Sons, a trading company, now occupies the 17th-century Government House, west of Old Gate at the corner of Church Street. At night the ghost of a young lady is to be heard creaking her way along in search of the dastardly Dutch soldier who jilted her. Across the street to the north stands the Dutch Reformed Church, built on the site of a Portuguese Capuchin monastery in 1755 to celebrate the birth of a son to the wealthy Dutch commander, Casparous de Jong. Inside are tombstones of the town's worthiest colonial servants, both Dutch and British.

Most elegant of the colonial buildings is next door, the **New Oriental Hotel** that served from 1684 as the Dutch Governor's offices. It was converted to a hotel just 50 years later, making it the oldest in Sri Lanka. Stop there at least for tea on the verandah and go upstairs for a view over the roofs and shady gardens of the fort. The 20th century just fades away.

Galle remains a major centre for artisans skilled in the working of tortoiseshell. The giant turtles of Sri Lanka have been declared an endangered species, but shells still arrive from the Maldive Islands. Small government-approved family-run "factories" operate

School buses are no fun when compared with a morning ride on the venerable bullock carts of Matara.

in near-by hamlets like KAN-DEWATTE.

Continue south-east along the coast road to **Koggala,** another gloriously lazy resort. Near the 83rd milestone (measured from Colombo), a road leads inland about 1½ miles to the **Buddhist temple** of KATALUWA. Ask your way carefully and you'll discover a marvellous group of 17th-century frescoes. They depict in almost comic-strip form episodes from Sri Lanka's spiritual and historical past. An English-speaking monk will be glad to explain the stories of Buddha's incarnation, the sad tale of Princess Patachara (and its happy ending), encounters with Portuguese overlords and an imaginary procession of Queen Victoria, added later.

Back on the coast, you'll pass the fishing village of **Weligama,** notable principally but not negligibly for the unique technique of its "stilt fishermen". For centuries, they've

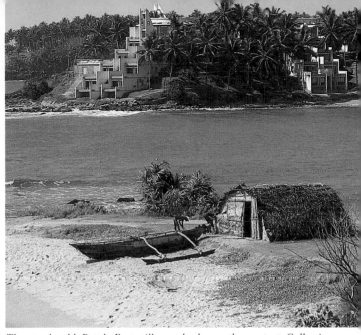

The sturdy old Dutch Fort still guards the south coast at Galle, in stark contrast to the ship-shaped hotel on the Tangalle promontory.

been doing an incredible balancing act perched on poles close to shore. They sit there for hours, catching, alas, very few fish. They say they just like the peace and quiet.

Matara, a former Arab trading post, might easily be dismissed as nondescript, its attractions gone the way of the once more lucrative gem and spice trade. But in fact it has a magnetic appeal for the modern visitor, however indefinable, and a wonderfully compelling atmosphere of life and movement. Abandon your car or bus and take a ride in one of the red upholstered carriages drawn by bullocks. **43**

These are not tourist gimmicks; they just happen to be the most comfortable way of getting around the narrow streets, as they have been for at least 600 years.

In the market, age-old focus of trade and still a thriving commercial centre, the merchants haggle with great humour. They're the descendants of traders who made the semi-precious zircon famous as the "Matara diamond". And they seem to do very well; their splendid bungalows overlook the ocean from the charming green hills surrounding the town.

One more pleasant resort lies further along the coast road: **Tangalla,** especially attractive because its shoreline is divided into intimate little bays, each with an expanse of dazzling white sand. And because of its distance from Colombo, Tangalla is much less crowded.

Continue along to **Hambantota,** a photogenic fishing village. Shoot your pictures from the promontory by the old colonial rest house overlooking the curving bay. The town was much favoured by tired British colonials for its bracing air. From here you can turn inland to Yala National Park (see p. 77).

Monsoons—Wet and Windy

For centuries, sailors in the Indian Ocean have charted their course by the monsoon, a wind that changes direction with the season. In Sri Lanka, the weather is affected by two different monsoons. Between November and February, heavy rains and high winds hit the north-east coast, while the south-west basks in sunshine. Conversely, rain pelts the south-west coast from May to September, when the north-east is dry and sunny.

The mechanics of the monsoon belong to the airy realms of meteorological science. Nonetheless, as the wind whips through your hair, it's interesting to know that differences in air pressure and temperature over the continental land mass of Asia and the Indian Ocean produce monsoons. The rotation of the earth also influences their formation.

In summer, the prevailing winds draw warm, moist air off the ocean, resulting in the heavy rains of the south-west. Downpours occur daily, often in the evening, but they rarely last very long. During the winter months, the winds shift, bringing the cool, dry air that gives rise to the less violent north-east monsoon. But however hard it may rain—it's always sunny somewhere.

East Coast*

The best time to go to the east coast, from Nilaveli to Batticaloa, is between May and September, when the south-west monsoon takes the fun out of bathing on the Colombo side of the island. The air is invigoratingly free of humidity and the beaches are a literally pure delight. But even between October and April, it's worth making a short trip.

On the east coast, the monsoon is much less fierce and unrelenting and, certainly from January on, you can have several carefree swimming days on clear, uncrowded beaches. In any case, the

Trincomalee is the age-old centre for shipping on Sri Lanka's east coast.

* At the present time, the resort of Trincomalee remains off limits to tourists. It's indispensable to make inquiries locally before planning an excursion anywhere approaching the strife-torn north-east.

east coast has not undergone the same intensive touristic development as the south-west and therefore offers a more restful holiday for those who want to get away from the madding crowd.

Several miles of beautiful beaches flank the small fishing village of **Nilaveli,** just north of Trincomalee. Not far from the village, Red Rock Beach, with its pink boulders and naturally blue paddling pools for the kids, makes a great target for family picnics. And the blue Sinnakarachchi Lagoon proves a haven of tranquillity; canny fishermen take their rods to the southern end, at the mouth of the river. Out to sea is Pigeon Island. The blue rock pigeons fared badly when the British Navy used the island for target practice, but the birds have gingerly made their way back and begun to breed again. You can watch spearfishermen making their dead-eyed catch and perhaps persuade them to let you try your hand.

On your way down to Trincomalee, make a side-trip about 6 miles west on the Anuradhapura road to the celebrated **Hot Wells of Kanniyai.** The Dutch enclosed this collection of seven hot springs in unattractive stone walls. The springs range in temperature from 93 to 104° Fahrenheit, as a guide on the spot will tell you. If you have rheumatism, there are several old men on hand to give you a healing shower of hot water scooped up in an ingenious, long-handled pail pierced with holes. Hindus swear by Kanniyai's soothing powers and the atmosphere is very cordial.

The principal attraction of **Trincomalee,** known popularly and universally as "Trinco", is **Koddiyar Bay,** one of the world's most magnificent natural harbours. Seasoned sailors place it right alongside San Francisco Bay and Rio de Janeiro's Guanabara; Lord Nelson himself said Koddiyar was quite simply the best. Trinco has been a port of call since the very dawn of Sri Lankan history.

The Tamils arrived not long after Vijaya set up his kingdom on the west coast over 2,000 years ago (see p. 13). Its strategic position in the Indian Ocean made Trinco a constant bone of contention between Portuguese, Dutch, French and British. In World War II, the British Navy was very concerned to defend it against Japanese bombs and an anti-aircraft gun emplacement can still be seen on Swami Rock.

The bay is sheltered to the north by the promontory on which the town of Trincomalee stands, and to the east by Foul Point, whose lighthouse is the fairest of sights for sailors coming in from the often stormy Bay of Bengal. The most enjoyable way to visit the port is on one of the excursion boats that leave from the Inner Harbour. Take

The Hot Wells of Kanniyai are said to provide cures for your aches. The Hindu Tamils have treated their rheumatism there for centuries.

a tour of Marble Bay, Dead Man's Cove and Coral Cove, perhaps stopping off at Sober Island for a picnic.

Trinco's town centre, predominantly Tamil, does not have a lot to offer. But drive out on the spit of land between Back and Dutch bays to **Fort Frederick,** built by the Portuguese in 1624. The fort, still a military establishment today, stands in a picturesque setting of banyan trees, with monkeys chattering aloft while spotted deer graze in the shade. But it is the **Hindu shrine**, or *kovil*, on Swami Rock that provides the major interest. Religious ceremonies are performed daily, with especially colourful ones on Friday evenings.

The Portuguese destroyed the original temple in the 17th century and threw its sacred statues into the ocean. Recently, an American diver recovered from the bay two bronze sculptures, of the god Vishnu and his wife Lakshmi, now on display outside the shrine. Believed to be more than a thousand years old, these sensual bronze nudes are usually covered with costumes, an in-

Trincomalee's shrine typifies the liveliness of Hindu architecture.

And Wellington to Boot

Shortly after the main gate on Fort Frederick Road in Trincomalee, you'll pass a large undistinguished house with a verandah. Sri Lankans pay it no attention, but you might like to know that it's Wellesley Lodge, where the Duke of Wellington stopped to convalesce from a tropical disease contracted during a campaign in India. His ship continued without him and sank with all hands in the Gulf of Aden. This enabled the Iron Duke to keep an appointment with Napoleon a few years later at Waterloo.

dication of present-day puritanism compared with the lustier freedom of an earlier age of Hinduism. Not far away, you can see another sculpture retrieved from the bay: a massive ancient lingam or phallus, symbol of Shiva, unadorned.

Swami Rock, which the god Shiva is said to have visited, has a more modern significance as a lover's leap. Legend says that a Dutch girl (not related to the benighted ghost of Government House in Galle) threw herself off the rock when the time came for her lover to jilt her, as Dutch lovers were wont to do when **49**

serving in Sri Lanka. Spoilsports claim that the girl in question in fact got married eight years after her supposed "leap". A little commemorative stone erected by her father does not say whether she jumped or not.

The second major east coast beach area includes **Kalkudah** and **Passekudah**, developed together like Beruwela and Bentota. Passekudah is protected by a reef, and swimming is gentle and easy in the off-monsoon season. **Batticaloa,** locally referred to as "Batti", stands on a peninsula almost separated from the mainland by a huge lagoon crossed by a ferry. The resort has a drowsy, timeless atmosphere that appeals to romantics.

Prawn fishing in the lagoon is an all-night torch-lit activity—with serenades from April to September by the **"singing fish"**. From the depths of the lagoon, you can hear a mysterious low drone and whine in which students of atonal music have heard affinities with Arnold Schönberg's *Sprechgesang* (word song), without the *Sprech.* Zoologists theorize that the source of the sound could be a school of catfish, shellfish lying on the bed of the lagoon or the tide running through empty mollusk shells.

Ancient Cities

A tour of the island's ancient cities is a journey through the history of Sri Lanka itself, as the rulers moved from one site to another in search of a secure site for the constantly beleaguered kingdom's capital. We can follow the movement over a period of centuries: from Anuradhapura, briefly to Sigiriya and then to Polonnaruwa, before the kingdom split up into several fiefdoms—finally coalescing in the face of the European enemy with a heroic last stand at Kandy (see pages 20–1).

The overriding force of the old capitals is the spiritual strength of Buddhism, exemplified in the age-old temples and powerfully serene statues of the Buddha himself. In fact many of the holy sites are still venerated by Buddhists. Visiting these ancient cities is a different experience from the pilgrimages we might make to European cathedrals, palaces and museums. By and large, the temples and other buildings are not so well preserved as their European counterparts. They have been subject not only to the ravages of internecine wars between Tamil and Sinhalese and wanton colonial destruction by the Europeans, but also to the erosions of the voracious tropical climate and the devastating invasion of the jungle.

And then there was the vogue for restoration and preservation during the fervent religious renewal of the 19th century, and a desire to "improve" on the original. But this should in no way deter you from touring the ancient cities. Bring to these places your own imagination and you'll be richly rewarded with a finer sense of Sri Lanka's past. You'll better understand the innate dignity of the Sinhalese and the Tamils, for both are present in the old capitals.

Anuradhapura

The island's first capital was established in the 4th century B.C. It was the citadel of the Vijaya dynasty, founders of the Sinhalese nation. The introduction of Buddhism there around the middle of the 3rd century B.C. made it the nation's spiritual capital, revered through all the changes of invasion and conquest down to the present day.

Today there are two Anuradhapuras, a modern town with the usual accoutrements of bank, post office, court house, hospital and railway station, and, to the north-west, the timeless ancient city of

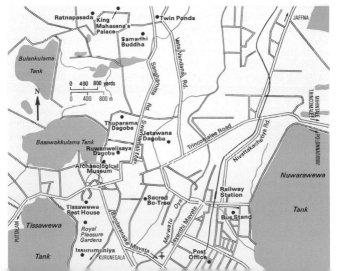

palaces, royal pleasure gardens, ritual bathing ponds and huge domed shrines that you see from afar—dazzlingly whitewashed or covered over with the grass and shrubs of centuries past.

To do the town properly, you really need an unhurried 24 hours, ideally from noon to noon. Begin at the **Tissawewa Rest House.** Even if you're not staying there overnight, it's one of the "musts" on the British colonial circuit and recognized as such by the Sri Lanka government, which is protecting it as a national monument. The elegant colonnaded building, set in a tree-shaded park greatly favoured by monkeys, provides a delightful setting for lunch. The rest house is named after the nearby Tissawewa Tank, the oldest of Sri Lanka's major reservoirs, built by King Tissa over 2,200 years ago to irrigate the rice paddies. It still functions. Strolling along the banks is pleasant in the evening.

Plan your tour of the ancient sites for the early morning hours of the next day and pay a visit to the instructive **Archaeological Museum**, signposted just east of the rest house. Museum guides will not only be glad to explain the collection but also, for a reasonable fee, to give you an informative and often amusing tour of the ancient city the next day. This is well worthwhile, as an unaccompanied tour can prove baffling and tiresome in the end.

The museum serves as a useful introduction to Anuradhapura's countless shrines, which are known by various names—*dagoba, vatadage* and *gedige.* Look for the interesting model of the Thuparama Dagoba, one of Anuradhapura's major monuments, showing how the temple was originally protected by a wooden roof and surrounded by a multi-pillared canopy. A brightly glittering golden casket is said to contain the ashes of King Dutugemenu, a heroic warrior of the 2nd century B.C. There are bronze and marble statues and 11th-century mural paintings from the sanctuaries and relic chambers. Compare the serenity of Buddhist sculpture with the voluptuous spirit of Hindu statuary from the 10th century—dancing four-armed goddesses and Ganesh the Elephant-god.

Outside the museum building you'll see a strange set of ornamental stones from the 5th and 6th centuries A.D. They are bidets, urinals and squatting-plates designed by a sect of Buddhist monks to show their scorn for the vanity of decorative art.

A full tour of the ancient city will take you to at least two dozen different sites. Here are the monuments you should not miss:

Ratnapasada (in the north-western corner of the ancient city). This ruin of an 8th-century Buddhist priest's palace is notable for its particularly fine "guardstone", a sculptural element commonly seen at the entrance to ancient Sri Lankan buildings. Standing under an arch with a kneeling elephant, the guardian figure is crowned with the protective symbol of the Naga, a seven-headed cobra. He carries a pot of lotus flowers in his one hand and a branch in the other, symbols of prosperity and plenty.

King Mahasena's Palace (immediately to the north). Important for another Sri Lankan sculptural speciality, the semi-circular "moonstone" on the floor of the entrance. The concentric bands or friezes sculpted in the stone are symbolic of aspects and stages of the spiritual life. An outer ring of flames represents the fiery core of the earth; the adjacent band carved with an elephant, horse, lion and bull symbolizes birth, disease, age and death; the wide floral frieze represents the life-force; then carrying lotus blossoms come geese, which stand for the power of intelligence, and the central lotus, symbol of Buddhist enlightenment.

Samadhi Buddha (to the east). A splendid seated image of the sage, widely regarded by scholars as one of the finest Buddha statues in the world. Try to see it very early in the morning when sunlight strikes the figure.

Twin Ponds (north-east corner). Marvellously restored 8th-century ritual baths. The water was brought several miles underground by an elaborate conduit system. Look in the far left-hand corner of the smaller pond, complete with filter and settling tank, and you'll see where the purified water poured through a spout beside a carved representation of the Naga.

Thuparama Dagoba (to the south). Oldest of the Anuradhapura temples, dating from the 3rd century B.C., it's said to house Buddha's collar-bone. Originally in a pointed, faintly pyramidal "paddy-heap" shape (like a heap of paddy rice), it was transformed during the 19th-century Buddhist revival to its present bell shape. The finely carved pillars **53**

that surround the temple supported a canopy like the one in the museum model.

Ruwanwelisaya Dagoba (to the north of the museum). A gigantic white temple built by order of King Dutugemenu in the 2nd century B.C., the shrine was the first to have the characteristic bubble dome.

The king's architects' competed to provide the design, which set the style for dagobas all over Sri Lanka. The winner got the commission by dropping water into a bowl, forming a bubble on the surface to demonstrate his chosen shape (altered in the 19th century).

Dutugemenu fell mortally ill during the construction and the builders covered the bubble-shaped scaffolding with white cloth to show the dying king how the completed shrine would look.

Today you'll see the devout placing offerings of lotus flowers and oil lamps at altars around the base of the dagoba. In addition to your morning visit, take a look at night if there's a good moon; the effect is spectacular.

Jetawana Dagoba (to the east). Anuradhapura's largest

The pillars around Thuparama Dagoba once supported a canopy.

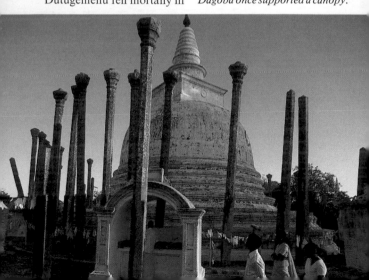

temple, originally nearly 400 feet high, and almost as big as Egypt's Great Pyramid. Now an overgrown ruin, it's an awe-inspiring example of the ravages of time being restored brick by brick as part of a large UNESCO programme.

Sacred Bo-Tree (south-east of the museum). The most holy object in Anuradhapura, attracting pilgrims all year round. It was grown from the tree under which Buddha achieved his enlightenment, and brought to Sri Lanka in 230 B.C. by Princess Sanghamitta, Prince Mahinda's sister. The prince had earlier introduced King Tissa to the Buddhist faith (see p. 15). The 2,200-year-old tree is protected in an enclosure beside a sanctuary.

Issurumuniya (south-west corner). Monastery with a nicely secular note in its delightful sculptures of Sinhalese aristocrats, cavorting elephants and, most celebrated of all, the **Gupta Lovers.** The lovers are said to be Prince Saliya and his wife Asokamala, a mere commoner. Eldest son of Dutugemenu, the prince—like the Duke of Windsor—gave up the throne for the love of his wife.

Royal Pleasure Gardens (beside Tissawewa Tank). Said to be the original site of the irreligious sculptures in the Issurumuniya. There are more cavorting elephants in the two pools and three lotus ponds of the park, fed originally from the Tissawewa reservoir.

Aukana

Travelling south-east from Anuradhapura on your way to Sigiriya and Polonnaruwa, it's worth making a detour to Aukana, site of one of the most impressive Buddha statues in Asia. The 40-foot standing sculpture was carved out of a granite monolith overlooking the Kalawewa Tank in the 5th century A.D. Once again, sunrise is the best time to see this colossal wonder. The pink rays of the morning highlight the statue's graceful features and perfect proportions, a miracle in a sculpture of this scale.

The **Aukana Buddha** is said to have been commissioned by King Dhatusena, a great builder of temples and reservoir tanks. This pious man was believed by his subjects to possess fantastic secret treasure. When he nominated his younger son to succeed him, the elder, Kasyapa, had him imprisoned and tortured to reveal the hiding-place of his fortune. Finally, near death, Dhatusena **55**

promised to deliver up his treasure if he were allowed to bathe one last time in the waters of his cherished Kalawewa Tank. There he lifted a handful of glistening water and offered it to his son and soldiers, saying: "This, my friends, is all the wealth I have." Kasyapa, in a fury, stripped his father naked, bound him in chains and had him walled up alive. Kasyapa fled to Sigiriya, and his father's treasure still sparkles in Aukana.

Sigiriya

The citadel built around A.D. 475 by the parricide King Kasyapa stands on the summit of Sigiriya, the "Lion Rock", undoubtedly the most spectacular monument in Sri Lanka. The massive fortress perches on top of a granite mountain hewn in the shape of a lion. Take courage and start the climb to Kasyapa's lair at sunrise. It's an adventure every visitor to Sri Lanka should attempt, and the ascent is by

no means arduous if you take it easy. Not only will you be rewarded with a magnificent panorama, but you'll also gain great insight into what Sri Lanka's warriors of old could conceive to protect themselves from their enemies—and from the curses of fate.

Go up towards the Lion's Paws (where there's a very welcome lemonade stand). Just before you reach them, you'll come to a steel spiral staircase. It leads to a gallery

Sigiriya's cloud maidens smile on the walls of the great Lion Rock.

decorated with a series of **frescoes** depicting 21 "cloud maidens" or "lightning princesses". The paintings in gentle orange, pink and green hues are the oldest, and probably most beautiful, in Sri Lanka.

The Mirror Wall protecting the gallery is glazed with a mysterious coating that archaeologists have partially identified as a mixture of honey, lime and egg white. Writing on it is of course strictly forbidden now, but for eight centuries, from about A.D. 600 on, visitors left their impressions of the lovely, mostly bare-breasted, girls in the frescoes. These **graffiti** are both an invaluable source for scholars studying the evolution of the Sinhalese language and most charming examples of the passing admirers' poetry. One proclaims: "Who is not happy when he sees those rosy palms, rounded shoulders, gold necklaces, copper-hued lips and long, long eyes?"

From the **Lion's Paws,** safely protected by a railing, you hug the rock face and take the very steps cut into the granite by Kasyapa's workmen. This was the way the king himself got up there. The steps lead through the lion's mighty throat to the summit, with ruins of the palace, a royal dance hall, the royal gardens,

baths and the king's granite throne. Down below, beyond the moated ramparts, you can see the fields where Kasyapa forsook his impregnable fortress to die by his own hand in 495.

Polonnaruwa

The 11th-century rulers of Sri Lanka left Anuradhapura in ruins and moved their capital to Polonnaruwa, 60 miles to the south-east. It was hoped that the distance and difficult terrain would make the new capital less prone to renewed attacks from the Indian mainland. For a while this proved to be true, and the next century was a golden age for Sri Lanka. Polonnaruwa developed into a magnificent city of palaces and temples, with the necessary status symbol of a splendid new reservoir. But the invasions resumed. Hindu influences in the architecture—and, indeed, Hindu temples among the Buddhist edifices—attest to the importance of Tamil conquests.

The venerable ruins that you'll see today, rescued from centuries of jungle overgrowth, bear eloquent witness to the struggles of empire builders. A walk among the crumbling structures of this medieval capital is quite a different experience from Anuradhapura. There are no modern restorations to jar the mood of reverie. You take a more contemplative journey back into Sri Lankan history.

Once again, it's a good idea to go around the ruins with a knowledgeable guide. The Archaeological Museum or nearby Ceylon Tourist Office will

The Gal Vihare Buddha is probably the greatest statue in Sri Lanka. **59**

POLONNARUWA

- Tivanka Image House
- Lotus Pool
- Gal Vihare

0   300   600 yards
0   300   600 m

Ancient City Wall
- Shiva Devale
- Vatadage
- Galpotha

Parakrama Samudra

Ancient City Wall

Rest House
Parakramabahu's Palace ● Audience Hall
Archaeological ● Museum
Ceylon Tourist Office
Royal Bath

Tank

Ancient City Wall

N ↑

- Parakramabahu Statue

help you find one. The museum is smaller and less essential than Anuradhapura's. Rather than providing an introduction to the city, it serves as a useful summary after your tour. For a preparatory or restorative cup of tea, visit the rest house beside the Parakrama Samudra Tank.

Here are some of the principal monuments to look for, working your way north:

Parakramabahu Statue (at the southern end of the site). The figure is thought to be carrying part of a rope symbolizing the "yoke of kingship". Although never definitively identified as representing the great 12th-century king, popular belief is overwhelmingly in his favour. Parakramabahu was the major builder of the capital, and his reservoir across the main road still bears witness to his constructive efforts for the kingdom's prosperity.

Parakramabahu's Palace Audience Hall and **Royal Bath** (due north of the king's statue). These buildings stand in noble ruin. Note the 10-foot thick palace walls and the jolly elephant frieze on the base of the audience hall platform.

Vatadage (in the section known as the Quadrangle). This circular relic house was originally covered by a wood-

en dome supported on stone pillars. There's a superb moonstone at the northern entrance to the upper terrace, with animal carvings more refined than those at Anuradhapura. The bull is notably absent from the friezes because strong Hindu influence by this time made the animal too sacred to step on. The more elaborate style of Polonnaruwa carving can be seen in splendid guardstones at the east entrance. On the temple wall there's an inscription claiming the building was put up by King Nissankamalla. But it is generally agreed this is the lie of a notorious braggart, and that the

The moonstones of Polonnaruwa are beautifully ornate thresholds of intricate symbolic significance.

temple is the work of his predecessor, the good Parakramabahu.

Galpotha (outside the Vatadage). The text of this stone "book" 27 feet long not only gives edicts on proper pious behaviour, but also tells us what a good chap Nissankamalla was. In addition, it relates the story of how the huge granite slab was removed over 60 miles from Mihintale by elephants pushing it on wooden rollers.

61

Shiva Devale (east of the Quadrangle). This Hindu temple was constructed during the 11th-century struggle for supremacy between Tamils and Sinhalese. In the central chamber are the stone lingam (male sexual organ) and yoni (female organ), major features of Hindu sanctuaries. The monkeys you'll see playing around the Shiva Devale are looked after by local zoologists and should not be fed.

Gal Vihare (to the north). Without doubt the highlight of any visit to Polonnaruwa, these four massive Buddha statues probably comprise the single most impressive collection of sculpture in Sri Lanka. Before inspecting them at close range, go up on the slab of rock that overlooks the monument from the east for an overall view. (On the rock you'll see a huge monolith that probably would have been used for further sculptures if work hadn't been interrupted by Tamil invaders.)

Looking at the Gal Vihare figures from left to right, you'll see first a seated Buddha in contemplation. Next, is another seated Buddha, preaching, with attendants. In the third sculpture, the Buddha is shown standing, looking sad and pensive. He is believed to be meditating on human suffering, a central concern of the creed. Last, 43 feet long, comes the reclining Buddha, passing at death into Nirvana. Taken as a whole, the monument expresses the quintessence of the Buddhist faith.

Lotus Pool and **Tivanka Image House** (further north). This delightful pool in the shape of an open eight-petalled lotus blossom draws its water from the reservoir by means of an underground conduit. It offered purification for visitors to the Tivanka Image House, which contains excellent frescoes. They depict the so-called Jataka tales of Buddha's previous incarnations in a style similar to the Sigiriya "cloud maidens". *Tivanka* is the name given to the distinctive "thrice-bent" pose of the Buddha, a gentle, relaxed attitude more usually associated with a female figure. Hindu influences show up in the frieze of unusually saucy dwarfs outside the shrine and, at the northern gate, in the female organ being impregnated by a bee. Buddhism does not inspire such frank sensuality.

Dambulla

Like nearby Sigiriya, Dambulla was a place of refuge—five caves on a mountain ledge occupied by King Valagam-bahu, who was driven out of Anuradhapura around 100 B.C. He recaptured his capital and in gratitude converted the caves into a temple.

The shrine is reached by an easy walk past a group of trinket stalls and lemonade stands. The most worthwhile of the five caves is the second. Facing into the far entrance of the **cave** is a statue of King Vala-gambahu, opposite statues of the Hindu gods Vishnu and Rama. (Sri Lankan Buddhism, the most tolerant of religions, incorporated the gods of other cults.)

Most interesting are the **frescoes** relating Buddha's struggles with the demon Mara, and the epic battle in the 2nd century B.C. between the Sinhalese hero-king Dutugemenu and his Tamil rival, Prince Elara. The painting on the ceiling sets out the sage's struggle with evil, ending triumphantly with the demon's elephant making obeisance to Buddha and, in the process, toppling the evil Mara over his shoulder.

If you're lucky enough to be there at sunset, look out from Dambulla at the wonderful play of shadow and light in the hills and plains of the surrounding countryside.

Kandy and the Hill Country*

The first joy of a visit to Kandy is the journey itself, whether you come by train or by road from Colombo or from the Ancient Cities region. As you rise into the hill country from the west, you pass through paddy-fields, rubber plantations and the first green slopes of tea plantations. You ascend eventually into a ring of granite mountains. Just before the town of KADU-GANNAWA, at about the 62nd milestone from Colombo, you'll enter a tunnel bored through solid rock. Kandyan tradition insisted that in order for the capital to be captured, the rock would have to be pierced. The British cut the tunnel after taking Kandy in 1815.

From the north, the road brings you up through the spice gardens of MATALE and across the Mahaweli, the river that loops around Kandy. By the Katugastota Bridge, you'll get a look at one of the town's

---

* Tourist visits to the area are allowed, though the region, and the Temple of the Tooth in particular, is patrolled by the military.

major tourist attractions, **elephants bathing** in the river. Most often you'll see one of them lying lazily on his side, obediently lifting a leg or raising the huge flap of an ear while his mahout or keeper soaps him down. These elephants spend much more time entertaining a happy public—Kandyans and tourists alike—with their ablutions than they do at anything so nasty as work lugging timber.

Kandy

Sri Lanka's proudest city courageously resisted the armed might of the Portuguese, the Dutch and the British, preserving the nation's identity while the rest of the country collaborated with colonial invaders. Without doubt, the Buddhist religion was the binding force. Sri Lanka's most sacred relic of the Buddha—the tooth rescued from the flames of his cremation at Kusinagara in

Elefacts

Since you'll be running into elephants all over the island —and hoping that none of them runs into you—you might like to be armed with a few facts about these awesome beasts.

To begin with, the elephant's trunk is not just a nose, it's also an upper lip. Elephants use their trunks to gather up to 400 pounds of food a day and 40 gallons of water, both for drinking and bathing. They go through three sets of molar teeth in a life that lasts up to 65 or 70 years. The baby is born after a gestation of 22 months and comes out a bouncing 180 pounds.

The elephant you'll see in Sri Lanka is the Asian variety, *Elephas maximus.* He's much smaller than his Afri-

can cousin, averaging some 9 feet high rather than 11 feet. But it's generally agreed he's better "designed", being nicely round and well-proportioned compared with the gangly, hump-backed *Loxodonta africana.*

More importantly, if you come across an elephant roaming in the wild, he'll usually give you a few hints about his intentions to charge. He stamps his forelegs and swings his ears at you, then he trumpets a mild protest, followed by a huge groaning roar. If you are still watching, look to see if he's tucked the tip of his trunk into his mouth; this means he intends to hit you hard. Most often, you'll be glad to know, he doesn't do this, because he's in fact just trying to scare you away. It frequently works.

India—lies in Kandy's Dalada Maligawa (Temple of the Tooth), symbol of national unity.

Today's town of 110,000 people preserves a distinctive architecture characterized by gently sloping tiled roofs, a feature which 20th-century architects aspire to incorporate in the modern urban landscape. Kandyan dancers and drummers have a style all their own and are a dominant element of religious festivals all over the country. But, above all, Kandy is an atmosphere, a spirit set apart from the rest of the island. Situated at an altitude of 1,000 feet, Kandy has a gentle climate, and its setting of hills, forest and lake combine to give the town an individual personality that must be appreciated at a leisurely pace.

The Colombo and Anuradhapura roads meet by Queen's Hotel at the north-west corner of the lake. Even if you're not staying there, the lobby makes a good place to stop and get your bearings out of the sun. The best overall

At bathtime in the Mahaweli River elephants are treated like kings.

view of town is from **Gregory's Road** on the other side of the lake, east of Royal Park.

Once you're rested, take a short, quiet walk around the lake, a decorative departure from the more utilitarian tradition of reservoir tanks. It's a relatively recent addition to the town, installed in 1807 by the last king of Kandy, Sri Wickrama Rajasinha. The island in the middle was Rajasinha's pleasure garden; for the British, who had other things on their minds, it served as an ammunition dump.

Take in the full sweep of the lake before arriving back at the northern shore and the **Dalada Maligawa,** the octagonal Temple of the Tooth. Close up, the building is not as spectacular as its prestige might have led you to expect (romantics should view it from

Drums and flutes greet the daily ceremony of Kandy's Sacred Tooth.

66

Gregory's Road). But you might like to attend the daily ceremonies of homage to the Tooth Relic held in the morning and at sunset. To a steady beating of drums, clashing of cymbals and wail of flutes, white-clad pilgrims carrying pink lotus blossoms and white frangipani approach the shrine. The air is filled with the scent of joss-sticks. A curtain is drawn aside to reveal, not the tooth, but a three-foot-high golden dagoba which itself holds another six, Chinese-box style, down to the innermost casket containing the relic. During the Kandy Esala Perahera, the most important ceremony of the Sri Lankan religious calendar, a replica of the shrine is carried through town on an elephant. *Esala* is a lunar month whose full moon falls in a period corresponding to our late July or early August; *perahera* means procession.

The Whole Tooth and Nothing but the Tooth

The Buddha's tooth, subject to plunder so many times over the ages, is revealed only on the rarest of occasions. Indian invaders repeatedly tried to steal it, the Portuguese attempted to burn it, destroying what the faithful insist was only a replica.

A British colonial official, Leonard Woolf (husband of novelist Virginia), insisted that he saw the relic while serving in Kandy before World War I. The tooth he was shown, wrote Woolf, "Whatever else it may be, has never been a human tooth. If my memory is correct, it is a canine tooth, about three inches long and curved." Of course, say the Buddhist scholars; the British, like the Portuguese, never did get to see the real thing.

The **National Museum,** east of the Dalada Maligawa, has a fine collection of Kandyan costumes, jewellery, weapons and beautifully carved tools. Among the exquisite ivory work, notice the umbrella handles, umbrellas being an important accessory in this land of heavy rain and hot sun. Look, too, for the deliciously frightening demon masks, much superior to the mass-produced models on sale in souvenir shops. There's also

The King of Kandy built himself a garden in the middle of the lake.

plenty of paraphernalia, often ornately decorated, for the still prevalent habit of betel-chewing. Besides leaving your teeth and gums scarlet, the mixture of aromatic leaf, areca nut, spices and chunam is said to induce a certain serenity. The decorative brass chunam boxes, nutcracker-like cutters for the areca nut and spatula-shaped betel-pounders hung from the necks of Kandyan nobles on chains. Larger boxes, for the addicted, were carried by servants.

On the hillside above town is the beautiful **Udawattekele Sanctuary,** a peaceful haven for bird life. The towering forest offers wonderful possibilities for walks and picnics.

You'll appreciate your stroll in the Udawattekele all the more if you first visit the marvellous **Botanical Gardens,** a few miles along the Colombo road at PERADENIYA. Start your tour early in the morning, as the gardens, covering some 150 acres in a loop of the Mahaweli Ganga, are worth at least a couple of hours of your time. Thousands of different trees and plants thrive here. Look out for the magnificent ficus grove, where the *Ficus elastica* spreads its low-slung branches and thick roots over a vast area. Or the African sausage tree with fruit like fat salami. Or the canonball tree with spherical flowers on its bark that explode into red bursts of petals.

Down by the river, clumps of giant bamboos from Burma and Malaya, their stems a foot in diameter, shoot up over 100 feet into the air. There are tamarind, magnolia, jasmine and orchid trees. And the spices—cardamom, cloves, cinnamon, nutmeg, vanilla, pepper and pimento—enough to persuade you that nothing cannot grow in Sri Lanka.

Continue along the Colombo road to the 65th milestone. From here you can make a nice little excursion through Kandy's back country, visiting three intriguing 14th-century temples and losing yourself for a while in the picturesque hills and valleys of the rice paddies lying peacefully off the beaten track. A sign points the way to the first temple, **Gadaladeniya,** standing on a forsaken rock outcrop. A couple of miles further on, at the top of a hill with a superb view over the valleys, is the **Lankatilake,** notable for its fine Kandyan roof and the stone elephant figures at the entrance to the outer wall. The most rewarding of the three temples is the **Embekke Devale,** charmingly situated at the end of a narrow village street. Notice the astoundingly well-preserved wood carvings on the pillars of its 600-year-old audience hall. The carved panels depict drunken dancers, wrestlers, soldiers, an elephant fighting with a lion and a touching scene of a mother feeding her baby with an older son at her side.

Nuwara Eliya

For anybody nostalgic or merely curious about the vestiges of British colonial presence that you inevitably stumble upon in the island's rest houses and Anglican churches, its ultimate manifestation is the hill station of Nuwara Eliya, a totally British creation. After the British moved in on Kandy, the army and colonial administrators set out to explore the surrounding countryside. In 1826, a hunting party came across the hill-top location of Nuwara Eliya, 48 miles from Kandy. At 6,000 feet, the air blowing off Pidurutalagala was cool and fresh, sweet with the scent of cypresses, eucalyptus and wild mint. Evergreens and yellow gorse covered the hillsides. Mountain streams gurgled by, just crying out to be stocked with trout. In the middle of sweltering Asia, God had given the British a piece of Scotland. Not only was it good hunting and fishing country, but also a place where they could cool off and recuperate from repeated bouts of malaria, dysentery and other tropical diseases contracted in the jungle and on the coastal plain.

By 1828, the hill station was set up to receive the convalescent servants of the empire. Some 20 years later, the explorer Sir Samuel Baker decided to settle there permanently; to stave off nostalgia for Britain, he made a perfect little English country town of Nuwara Eliya. You can still see the result, a mixture of Tudor, Georgian and Queen Anne architecture, gabled roofs, bow windows, cross-beamed walls. The gardens have immaculate lawns with rose bushes and herbaceous borders surrounded by privet hedges. The moss-covered gravestones of the churchyard are worthy of Thomas Gray's elegy. The post office has a very English clock tower.

Enjoy Nuwara Eliya, then, for its quaintest of quaint atmospheres, the spectacular setting of the 18-hole golf course, walks in the surrounding woods. Visit **Hill Club,** complete with billiard room, polished oak dining room, portraits of Winston Churchill and Queen Elizabeth and *Country Life* magazines in the reading room. The roaring log fire in the evening is every bit as welcome as the one woollen sweater you should have brought to Sri Lanka.

Going to work in a rice-paddy is a muddy but not miserable business.

An overgrown racecourse and paddocks lie at the southern edge of town, another sweetly melancholy reminder of the old days. Now only a few infrequent pony races are held. The road past the racecourse leads 6 miles to **Hagkala Botanical Gardens,** less spectacular than Kandy's, but charmingly landscaped for long, cool walks, perhaps with a picnic at the end in one of the pavilions overlooking the valley.

But Nuwara Eliya is more than a homesick Englishman's dream come true. It's also a centre for the flourishing tea industry. As you make the lovely drive from Kandy, after the bridge at GAMPOLA, you will curve up through the luscious green **tea plantations.** Fields of tea carpet the hillsides, irrigated by cascades of rain water. Bobbing their heads above the tea bushes are the pickers, who daintily pluck with their fingertips a bud and two leaves of each new growth and toss them into the baskets on their backs. They pass each bush at 20-day intervals. From Nuwara Eliya, your hotel can arrange a tour of a tea factory, where you can view the fermenting, drying and sorting processes that go into producing your favourite blend.

Hill Country Sights

HORTON PLAINS, south of Nuwara Eliya, offers a hiker's delight: the 2½ mile walk from a rest house named Farr's Inn to **World's End,** one of the great scenic wonders of the island. This cliff drops down 5,000 feet, providing a fantastic view over the south-

ern coastal plain to Hambantota early in the morning. A
negotiable path leads 7 miles
past mountain streams and
clear pools to a main road at
BELIHUL OYA.

The less hardy traveller will
prefer his beautiful view of the
southern plain from **Ella Gap,**
an easy drive east from Nuw-

*The cool tea plantations offer a
change from the hot coastal plain.*

ara Eliya via BANDARAWELA.
From the rest house terrace
at Ella, you can look down
past the sparkling Rawannah
Ella Falls (where the demon
Rawannah is said to have held
the goddess Sita captive in a

cave), over to Yala National Park (see p. 77).

From the end of December to April—the clear, gentle season—Buddhist, Hindu and Muslim pilgrims converge on Hatton, Maskeliya and Dalhousie (south-west of Nuwara Eliya) to make the 4-mile walk up the steps leading to 7,362-foot-high **Adam's Peak**. At the top is a rock with a hollow shaped like a human footprint. Muslims believe that Adam stood there in expiation of his sin in the Garden of Eden. Buddhists claim that it was Buddha who left the mark during a visit to the island, while Hindus hold the print to have been made by the god Shiva during the Dance of Creation.

From the peak, in the clear light of dawn, you can see the lighthouses of Colombo Harbour, Galle and Dondra Head. Turn around and you'll see the lighthouse of Foul Point at Trincomalee on the other side

of the island. But the most spectacular sight of all is the **"Shadow of the Peak".** The north-east winds of the pilgrim season blow a bank of clouds into the valley below and for a brief moment, the rising sun casts the mountain's giant triangular shadow onto the cloud mass. As the sun rises, the triangle shrinks and moves towards you, losing itself finally in the rocks.

If you plan your visit carefully, you can see this phenomenon without difficulty. Travel via HATTON to DALHOUSIE in the afternoon. Stock up with a flask of tea and sandwiches and make your way up towards the Japanese temple recently built en route. You can rest overnight either at the temple itself or in one of the many tea houses on the way. The last steep climb from

Seek treasure in jewels at Ratnapura or the Shadow of Adam's Peak.

the temple should begin at least an hour before dawn to give you time to get in place for the great moment, what the White House press corps knows as a "Major Photo Opportunity".

On the way back to Colombo from Nuwara Eliya, via Ella, gem enthusiasts will want to visit **Ratnapura,** literally "City of Gems", where most of Sri Lanka's precious, semi-precious and outright fake stones are cut and polished (see p. 90). Some of the stones are mined from gem pits along the road between Pelmadulla and Ratnapura. You can watch workers go down some 30 feet to the stratum of the earth where the gems are usually found. They scoop out the pebbly soil, containing, they hope, the odd sapphire, ruby or garnet or two. The stones are taken back to Ratnapura, where they are cut and polished in the doorways of back-street workshops. East of town there's a **Gemmological Museum** (also a commercial establishment) where you can examine jewels from all over the world, without any undue pressure to buy the locally produced merchandise. Ask the friendly director how to recognize a fake and he will reply: "Expertise."

National Parks

Although most of Sri Lanka's wildlife reserves are largely inaccessible to visitors, two extensive national parks—Yala in the south-east and Wilpattu on the north-west coast—provide facilities for photo safaris. There are bungalows inside the parks (make reservations through the Department of Wildlife in Colombo) and hotels on the immediate outskirts. You should tour the parks early in the morning or late in the afternoon, during hunting and feeding hours; at other times, the animals retire into the jungle to sleep.

Yala

For a general impression of the park, spend the night at a hotel or rest house in nearby TISSAMAHARAMA and make your drive through the half-savannah, half-jungle terrain early in the morning. Buses and four-wheel-drive vehicles are available for hire, with a ranger as guide.

Bird-watchers will be rewarded with the loveliest of peacocks, jungle fowl, black-necked storks, pelicans, herons, spoonbills, pupu birds and pea-green bee-eaters. Also keep your eyes open for spotted and sambur deer, wild boar, buffalo, crocodiles and, of course, elephants. The one creature that any alert visitor to Yala can spot is the deft little dung beetle, who scampers along backwards, pushing with his hind legs a dried ball of animal dung three times bigger than himself.

Life in the Yala National Park is a pleasant romp for the elephants, better than hauling timber around a building site on the west coast.

With extraordinary luck—don't let anybody persuade you it's easy—you may catch a glimpse of the island's most elusive animal, the leopard. The most likely place is Wepandeniya Leopard Rock. For a serious chance, you must stake out the area from a bungalow. This is a delightful experience in itself, offering a more leisurely view of the animals and birds in their enchanting natural environment.

Wilpattu

This vast reserve appeals to wildlife enthusiasts prepared to spend a couple of nights in a bungalow inside the park. The best time to go is from May to August, when dry weather forces animals out to the open water holes. Your chances of seeing a leopard in Wilpattu are slightly better than in Yala, because he tends to hunt in the daytime here. The park's other speciality is the deceptively cuddly-looking sloth bear, which feeds, like Pooh, on honey. This creature has a vicious temper. He can run at considerable speed when challenged by interlopers and produces incredible screams and groans when aroused by a mama bear in the mating season.

The Maldives

To look at, the Maldives are all the treasure islands you ever read or dreamt about as a child, set in a sea bluer and clearer than natural waters have any right to be. This sun-soaked land lies 450 miles south-west of Sri Lanka in the Indian Ocean. For the sheer self-indulgence of lazing in the tropics, with deep-sea diving for the more energetic, there's nowhere better. The Maldive Islands make an excellent icing on your Sri Lanka holiday cake.

Some 1,200 islands, reefs and sand banks constitute the 19 atolls of the Republic of the Maldives. The island-clusters extend 500 miles from north to south and 180 miles from east to west at their widest point. About 200 islands are inhabited with a total population of around 200,000; about 65 are set aside for tourists, separate from those occupied by Maldivians. Each island is so small that it serves just one function. There's an island for the airport, Hulule, another for the republic's capital, Male, a third for the prison, and so on. Some are only just above sea-level.

You may find the people on

the capital island a little less easy-going than the Sri Lankans, but in the fishing villages, after an initial shyness, they will show you a great generosity and warmth in the deep-rooted tradition of Muslim hospitality.

A Brief History

The atolls—a word of Maldivian origin—are believed to be the protusions of a submerged land mass that includes the Laccadive Islands to the north and the Chagos Islands to the south. An upheaval pushed the islands and coral reefs above the ocean surface not more than 100,000 years ago.

Like Sri Lanka, the earliest inhabitants of the Maldives came from southern India. They were joined around the 5th century B.C. by another wave of colonizers from the north.

Recorded contact with the outside world didn't begin until the first Arab traveller passed through in 947. The Maldives later provided a useful station for the trade in spice, pearls, coconuts and dried fish, as well as a superabundant supply of cowrie shells, the accepted form of currency from Africa to China until the 16th century.

In 1153, Sultan Mohammed

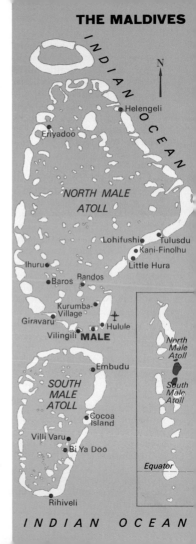

THE MALDIVES

INDIAN OCEAN

N

Helengeli
Eriyadoo

NORTH MALE ATOLL

Lohifushi Tulusdu
Kani-Finolhu
Ihuru Little Hura
Baros Randos
Kurumba-Village
Giravaru Hulule
Vilingili MALE

Embudu

SOUTH MALE ATOLL

Cocoa Island
Villi Varu
Bi Ya Doo

Rihiveli

North Male Atoll
South Male Atoll

Equator

INDIAN OCEAN

Ibn Abdulla converted to Islam and all the inhabitants became officially Muslim, though vestiges of Buddhism remained at the outer northern and southern limits of the archipelago. Here, in defiance of official edicts, the Buddhist statues and dagobas were left covered with earth, but not destroyed.

The Maldivians stayed free of foreign intereference until the Portuguese arrived in 1512. The Europeans pursued the same brutal policy as in Sri Lanka, but Sultan Thakuru Faanu formed a powerful alliance with Indians from the Malabar coast and totally wiped out the Portuguese force in 1573. In succeeding centuries, the Malabaris tried to exact too great a debt of gratitude, and the aid of the French was enlisted in 1754 to ward them off. For a change, French soldiers didn't stay long, being preoccupied with a little disturbance of their own in 1789.

But the protection racket resumed in 1887 with the British, who offered their services in exchange for an annual tribute and exclusive use of the southernmost island of Gan. This became a Royal Air Force base in 1957 and was relinquished only in 1976.

The Maldives entered the United Nations as a fully independent nation in 1965, the present republic being proclaimed in 1968. The first president was the authoritarian Ibrahim Nasir, who was deposed in 1978 and succeeded by a more fundamentalist Islamic government. Today the economy has moved well beyond cowrie shells to a growing tourist industry and large-scale fish-processing in factories installed by the Japanese.

What to See

Each of the islands developed for foreign visitors is a self-contained tourist resort administered by a hotel, with bungalows, restaurant, bar, sports facilities and shops. When you arrive at your hotel (by a sea-plane or motor-launch that meets you at the airport), you'll probably want to take a walk around your island to get your bearings. Within a few minutes, you'll come across a set of buildings that look surprisingly similar to the ones you just left. This is not another hotel, it's *yours*. You've made a complete tour of the island.

Nobody's ever accused visitors to the Maldives of being workaholics.

Once you have tried scuba diving in the Indian Ocean, you may never want to go back to swimming pools.

For most people, this is a cosy feeling. But if you find it oppressively restricting, there are plenty of opportunities to get out and around. The hotels organize island-hopping excursions to the best Maldivian-inhabited islands, where you can visit **fishing villages.** You're likely to receive a friendly invitation to the fishermen's homes, where you may be offered a cup of sweet tea and a spicy fish cake. You can also explore totally uninhabited islands, barbecue the fish you might have caught on the way, or at least picnic on the packed lunch provided by the hotel.

The resort islands do not differ greatly one from the other. Dazzling white-sand beaches, palm trees, bungalows, tennis courts are common to all. Construction on the islands dates from 1972, the year the Maldives were opened up to tourism, so there is no historic "sightseeing" apart from Male. The most interesting sights are underwater: the fish that can be observed while snorkelling or scuba-diving. Sharks, giant turtles, barracuda, spiny lobster and pilot-fish more than make up for the lack of palaces, temples and museums.

Some resort islands are noted for their wide range of aquatic sports facilities. Others (those favoured by the French!) are known for their superior cuisines. Yet others are unpretentious, but have created an especially friendly atmosphere. But all have in common beautiful shores and startlingly clear waters.

Male is interesting mainly for the port, the closest thing to bustling activity in the Maldives. Government offices front the harbour, and boats constantly come and go with important-looking official packets for the outer islands. Larger boats bring in provisions for the hotels; nearly everything but fish and coconuts has to be imported from Colombo or Singapore. The fishing fleet returns with the catch early in the morning and late in the afternoon. The fish are sold in the market at the west end of the harbour, but in your drowsy Maldivian state of mind, you may find the haggling too strenuous to watch.

Away from the harbour, the town is a sleepy cluster of blinding white-washed houses with high-walled gardens. The streets are of baked earth. West of the imposing Presidential Palace is peaceful **Sultan's Park.** The painstakingly nurtured lawns, flower beds and sculptured bushes seem to need watering all day long, the rains here rarely being very long-lasting or heavy.

The nearby **museum** is worth a visit for the display of sultans' thrones and costumes, but above all for the fascinating *Kema Kolhu*. This four-cornered tent, which was borne through the streets of Male by palace servants, protected ladies of the royal household from the stares of the populace when they walked through town. While women remain modest generally, today you'll see plenty out on the streets of Male.

But don't feel guilty if you, too, prefer to stay off the streets, relaxing in the sun on your island. For foreigners, indolence in the Maldives is not a sin.

Maldives Briefing

Airport. Hulule Airport occupies an island to itself, a mile from Male. Expansion of the airport complex now enables Hulule to accommodate large jets. Boats transport passengers to nearby Male and all the resort islands. A departure tax is charged.

Currency. Maldivian *rufiya* (Rf) and *laari* (L). Issued in 2, 5, 10, 20, 50, 100 and 500 rufiyaa; 1, 2, 5, 10, 25 and 50 laari.

Dress. T-shirts and shorts of a respectable length are acceptable wear for tourists, but trousers for men and skirts for women are preferred. Nudity on the beach is a punishable offence.

Drugs. The import of drugs into the Maldives and their use in the islands are against the law. Even minor offences result in severe punishment.

Electric Current. 220 volts.

Emergencies. In Male, dial 119 for police; 118 for fire; 102 for an ambulance.

Entry Regulations: Valid certificates of vaccination against yellow fever are required of all travellers arriving from or transiting infected areas.

Hospital. Central Hospital, Male; tel.: 322400, Facilities suitable only for minor problems. Flying Swiss Ambulance provides a 24-hour emergency clinic for tourists; tel.: 324508, 324500; telex 77089 FSA MF; fax: 324509.

Hours. Businesses open 7.30 a.m. to 1.30 p.m., Saturday to Thursday.

Public Holidays. *Fixed dates:* New Year's Day (1 January), Independence Day (26–27 July), Victory Day (3 November), Republic Day (11–12 November). *Movable dates based on Islamic calendar:* National Day, Prophet Mohammed's Birthday, Huravee Day, Martyr's Day, Beginning of Fasting Season, Fithr Eid Day, Hajj Day, Alh'a Eid, Hijree New Year.

Residence. Everyone entering the Maldives should preferably have a confirmed hotel reservation.

Taboos. The import of alcohol, pork, pornographic material and idols are strictly prohibited, though alcohol is available on the resort islands. Tourists cannot enter Male after 10 p.m.

Tourism Information Unit. Ministry of Tourism, Male; tel.: 325528; telex: 66019 TOURISM MF; fax: 322512.

What to Do

Sports

Since Sri Lanka and the Maldives are islands, the dominant leisure activity, at least for foreign visitors, is naturally enough **swimming.** In the Maldives, the resort islands have been chosen with care and it's safe to swim around any of them. Take the usual precautions when swimming from a boat, especially beyond a coral reef where currents can be treacherous.

On the beaches of Sri Lanka, you must be a little more prudent, even in the most popular resorts. Watch out for red warning flags indicating dangerous currents or unfavourable seas at Negombo, Beruwela and Bentota, though conditions there usually prove quite safe. Mount Lavinia is risky. Go instead to excellent, reef-protected Hikkaduwa. On the lovely beaches of Tangalla, you just have to be careful which little bay you choose; some are as calm as a pond in a park, others conceal jagged rocks and whipping undercurrents. On the east coast, Nilaveli and Passekudah both have good safe beaches. Failing all else, most hotels are equipped with swimming pools.

Snorkelling and **scuba-diving** are good at Hikkaduwa, justly famous for its coral sanctuary. You swim among gorgeous tropical fish scarcely more colourful than the multi-hued coral reef that marks their protected area. Equipment and lessons are available at the hotels, and diving clubs arrange excursions to offshore shipwrecks. The diving is also very good around Pigeon Island (off Nilaveli) and at Passekudah.

But the experts all agree that the best diving in the region— some would say in the Maldives— is to be found in the Maldives. Discovered by Italian enthusiasts, the islands offer face-to-face encounters with barracudas, turtles, and, they say, harmless schools of sharks. The equipment on Bandos is the most modern, including decompression chambers for deep-sea diving.

Back in Sri Lanka, there's some reasonable **surfing** at Hikkaduwa, good **water-skiing** in the lagoon at Bentota, and **windsurfing** everywhere.

Sailing is being developed in the Maldives, but the British left the sport well established **85**

in Sri Lanka, with clubs in Colombo harbour (Colombo Yacht Club) and on Bolgoda Lake (Colombo Motor Yacht Club) south of the city. Try your hand at **rowing,** particularly pleasant on Kandy Lake. Rowing clubs in Colombo and Kandy provide equipment.

Fishing is a major Sri Lankan pastime, and as varied an activity as you could wish. On the coast there's estuary fishing, an all-year affair, except for the high monsoon months of June and July on the west coast and November–December on the east. Go after barracuda, queen-fish and estuary perch at the southern end of Negombo's lagoon and in Nilaveli's Sinnakarachchi Lagoon. **Spear-fishing** for queen-fish, yellowfin barracuda and giant grouper is a Trincomalee speciality (February to September), but there's also very good sport on the west coast at Negombo, Bentota, Beruwela, Galle and Tangalla (November to April). For **deep-sea fishing,** Trinco can't be bettered; the Sea Angler's Club provides boats and tackle for tuna, marlin, swordfish, sailfish and shark (March to October). In the Maldives, **deep-sea fishing** is a romantic adventure, as boats set out after sunset. It all
86 ends, you hope, with a midnight barbecue of the catch.

River fishing is best on the west side of Sri Lanka in March and April, and again in August and early September. On the east side, you can go out all the year round. Sporting anglers hope for a bout with the fighting mahseer, usually around 3 pounds, but

growing up to 25. Try your luck on the Mahaweli at Katugastota, north of Kandy—one of the best spots. The Ceylon Fishing Club organizes **trout fishing** in the mountain streams around Nuwara Eliya and Horton Plains. Apply for a licence at the Hill Club in Nuwara Eliya.

Sports Ashore

Hunting for wild boar is very much encouraged by sugar planters, anxious to protect their cane fields from marauding herds. The Sugar Corporation will be glad to help hunters set up a shoot at Kantalai, inland from Trinco. Snipe and duck shoots are popular in rice

country and at coastal lagoons. If you take the coast road to Wilpattu and Anuradhapura, stop and try your luck for duck at the salt flats of Puttalam.

Sri Lanka offers two fine 18-hole **golf** courses, the Royal Colombo Golf Club and the Nuwara Eliya, one of the most spectacular courses in the world. There the "rough" ends in the jungle; "hazards" include trout streams and three holes carved out of a mountain, known collectively as "Switzerland". At over 6,000 feet above sea level, you'll need a warm sweater and a very good iron to combat the valley wind.

If **tennis** is your game, be sure to play early in the morning or late in the afternoon. Most good hotels have courts, but you have to watch out for the grass that seems, in this tropical climate, to grow up between the cracks in the hard courts while you're changing ends after the first set.

Getting around on a windsurf board made for one or a bicycle for two.

Of the spectator sports, **cricket** is by far the most popular, baffling as it may be for those without a British or Commonwealth upbringing. Sri Lankans look much more handsome than Englishmen in correct cricket wear and seem to combine the necessary dignity and enthusiasm with great flair. For beginners, there's often a casual game underway on Galle Face Green in Colombo.

One sport that everyone can do, **bicycling**, couldn't be more delightful along the banks of the old Dutch canals that parallel the coast in the Negombo area, or around the Tissawewa Tank at Anuradhapura (see pp. 109–110). **89**

Shopping

Most of Sri Lanka's best shopping is concentrated in Colombo. Craftsmen from all over the country send their goods to the metropolis, where they have the greatest chance of making a sale to foreign visitors. Jewellers, goldsmiths and curio and mask shops abound in the Pettah and Fort areas, but prices aren't fixed. The more adventurous bargain hunters will have to shop around for the best buy.

If you prefer to play it safe, to be sure that your gems are genuine and your tortoiseshell or ivory is not a clever plastic imitiation, stick to the state-run Laksala shops and the State Gem Corporation. Apart from their main offices in Colombo, the state corporations have branches in all the major resorts. They also operate boutiques in many hotel lobbies. You will frequently, though by no means always, get a better price at a privately owned shop, but you won't have the government guarantee of genuine merchandise.

In light of the colonial plundering of the past 400 years, there is now a ban on the export of antiques (objects dating from before the 20th century).

Best Buys

Gems have been a prime target for visitors to Sri Lanka since Marco Polo marvelled at the island's rubies. Most of the precious stones are mined in the Ratnapura district (see p. 76). You can inspect them in a mounted and unmounted state before making your choice, there or elsewhere. Prices vary, not only in terms of quality but also of fashion, with rarity playing more of a role than mere beauty. For instance, the aesthetically unexceptional alexandrite fetches a higher price than the prettier but more common wine-red garnet. The alexandrite's value derives from its unique capacity of changing from emerald green in daylight to red under artificial light.

At the top end of the scale, and not likely to lose their desirability, are sapphires and rubies, second in hardness only to diamonds. The 400-carat "Blue Belle" sapphire in the crown of Queen Elizabeth of England came from Sri Lanka. Sapphires here are not only blue, but also a very attractive yellow. Rubies

Choose either a frightfully funny doll or a delicately polished gem.

range from an exquisite pink through delicate violet to rich pigeon-blood red. These stones often have an "inclusion" (a particle of foreign matter) which, far from being a flaw, is considered an enhancing feature, producing what experts call an "asterism" or star effect when held against the light.

Diamonds are not found in Sri Lanka, but there are semi-precious zircons. These are brilliant enough in appearance, but soft, passing as a diamond only with a medieval Matara trader's gift of gab, hence the nickname "Matara diamond". A much better bargain is the yellow topaz—hard, highly polished, a delight to touch and behold. Watch out for smoky quartz, a nice enough stone, but sometimes palmed off as "smoky topaz". In fact, in general, watch out!

The State Gem Corporation will examine, free of charge, gems purchased elsewhere but if they prove to be fakes, the Corporation can do nothing to help you get your money back.

Sri Lanka has taken over the old Javanese art of batik-dyeing and added its own exquisite designs.

Of course, if you're an expert, you have nothing to fear.

Sri Lanka specializes in two forms of fine craftsmanship that challenge modern ecological sensibilities: objects of **ivory** and **tortoiseshell.** The elephants and turtles that provide these materials are both protected species, but the goods alas still keep coming through. The inhabited islands of Himmafushi, Maafushi and Gulhi of Male atoll and some of the outer islands today produce articles of repute from tortoise shell, coral stone, fish bone and coconut shells.

The trouble is that Sri Lankan workmanship is superb and difficult to resist. The Laksala shops and other respectable concerns sell ivory bangles, necklaces and sculptures and tortoiseshell jewellery, handbags and other items (a speciality of the Galle area) with the warning that they may be confiscated by customs officials. In practice, this just doesn't happen at Colombo Airport, but customs officials in stricter countries such as the United States do regularly seize ivory and tortoiseshell goods. If you do decide to buy something, the test of authenticity is simple: ask the salesman to hold a lighted match to the object. The plastic will

The Old-Fashioned Way

Sri Lankan craftsmen imported the ancient art of batik from Indonesia. This painstaking method of printing designs on textiles came down from the Egyptians and Sumerians; the word means "wax painting" in Javanese.

An artisan traces a pattern in wax on both sides of a piece of silk or cotton with a brush or copper tool. Sometimes, to speed things up, the designs are printed assembly-line fashion by wooden blocks dipped in wax. But this isn't true batik.

After it has been coated with wax, the cloth is dipped in dye and left to dry If the wax cracks and the dye seeps through, a desirable "crackle" effect results. The wax may be wholly or partially scraped away, depending on the design, and a second coat applied before the cloth is dyed again. This process is usually repeated many times with different colours. Silk can be worked with little preliminary treatment, but cotton requires extensive preparation.

In Sri Lanka, you'll find batik designs in many shapes and forms. They make it into lampshades, curtains, bedspreads, pillows and wall hangings. And, of course, it's also meant to be worn for all to admire.

melt, but the real thing will emerge unharmed. Most often, it never gets that far. A faker will refuse the test.

Masks used in pageants and village dramas make popular souvenirs, though most of them are mass-produced and grotesque in quite the wrong way. Look for the honourable replicas of Naga (demon-snake) or royal Kolam masks produced in the workshops of **Ambalangoda**, some of which reach Colombo.

Modern handiwork includes **batik** textiles, a skill successfully imported from Indonesia and adapted by Sri Lanka craftsmen; highly decorative **rag dolls;** and the **basketware** of Jaffna. If you have the urge to "go native", you can buy lovely **saris.** For unisex wear, pick up some of the cool, billowing **cotton shirts** and **baggy trousers** for sale in the pavement bazaar at Hikkaduwa. They're ideal for loafing, and cheap.

Nightlife and Folklore

Nightlife in the resorts means the inevitable discotheques, beach barbecues and moonlight cruises on the lagoon. Colombo has a growing number of casinos, some with nightclubs, and a visit to the cinema can be an experience. Sri Lankan films have a sense of the romantic that makes a Hollywood love story of the 1930s seem very tepid by comparison.

Folklore displays, on the other hand, are usually boisterous and knockabout. Kandyan and low country dancing can be seen on the stage or, best of all, in *poya* religious festivals and *perahera* pageants celebrated by Buddhists and Hindus throughout the year. The dances exorcize devils, celebrate popular animal figures

Roadside batik boutiques in Hikkaduwa and a pre-punk pukka Hindu.

such as the lion or elephant, and reenact myths and legends like that of the goddess Devadatta and the swan Hansa, not unlike the Greek myth of Leda and the Swan. Other dances are more spiritual, such as the *vannama*, which expresses the serenity of Buddha, and the *dahata sanni*, invoking the spirits of 18 human qualities—among them greed and malice, but also joy and carnal love.

The dancers, mostly men, perform to a great pounding of drums and cymbals in grotes-

Elephants are lit up like a birth-day cake for full moon festivals.

que, frightening or humourous masks. They wear elaborate costumes and often have rings on their fingers and bells on their toes. They fling themselves around with considerable agility and energy, demonstrating, particularly in the stick and sword dances, impressive feats of acrobacy.

Calendar of Events

January   *Duruthu Perahera.* Pageant held at Kelaniya Temple, not far from Colombo, in celebration of a visit by Buddha to Sri Lanka.

Thai Pongal. Hindu harvest festival in homage of the sun god.

February   *Independence Day.* On the 4th, a national holiday.

March/April *New Year.* Both Sinhalese and Tamils celebrate with elephant races, coconut games and pillow fights

Easter. Catholics perform a Passion Play at Duwa, on Negombo lagoon.

May   *Vesak.* Most sacred full moon festival. Commemorates the birth, enlightenment and death of Buddha. The streets are gaily decorated with paper lanterns and clay coconut-oil lamps.

June   *Poson.* Full moon festival celebrating Prince Mahinda's bringing of Buddhism to Sri Lanka (see pp. 13–15). Especially colourful at Anuradhapura.

July/August *Kandy Esala Perahera.* The biggest pageant of the year, lasting 11 days, with richly costumed elephants, torch-bearers, dancers, drummers and whip-crackers.

Vel. Hindu festival in honour of the war god Skanda, whose gilded chariot is paraded through the streets of Colombo from the Pettah to Bambalapitiya.

December   *Sangamitta.* Full moon festival celebrating the arrival in Anuradhapura of a cutting from the Sacred Bo-Tree over 2,000 years ago.

Dining Out

Most hotel managers assume that foreign visitors to Sri Lanka don't want to sample the local culinary specialities. Many years of experience with complaints from timid tourists too abruptly surprised by exotic changes in their normal diet have persuaded them it's safer to provide a bland "international" cuisine of grilled or stewed meats and fish with boiled or fried vegetables. These dishes are often presented as quasi-French—"veal cordon bleu"—or nostalgic British—"Brown Windsor soup" and "Scotch eggs". The one concession to local tastes is the unavoidably exotic fruit available for breakfast, lunch and dinner. Even here, too many establishments play it safe (and cheaper) with bananas and pineapples—tasty enough, but not exactly an adventure.

But there is a way out. Hotel menus often offer an unspecified "curry of the day". This is your chance. Talk to the manager ahead of time, ask to see the chef, and discuss with them the possibility of having an authentic Sri Lankan meal. They will be delighted to oblige. You may not want spicy curries every day, but you should know that you can, with a little initiative, get away from meat and two vegetables.

Meal Times
Lunch is served from 12 to 2 p.m., dinner from 7 to 9 p.m. (later in Colombo).

Restaurants
The Sri Lankans themselves generally go out to eat only when they're away from home. In Colombo, there are few luxury restaurants specializing in native cuisine, but rather popular eating houses that cater to Sri Lankans in search of simple food for a reasonable price. To enjoy Sinhalese cooking at its best, you need an invitation to dine at home with local people. Outside Colombo, many guest houses and rest houses serve excellent curries and other specialities.

Eating Habits
Most Sri Lankans eat with their fingers, but foreigners needn't follow suit. The restaurants that cater to tourists will gladly provide knives and forks. At a typical restaurant, an array of small dishes will be placed on your table. You serve yourself, filling your bowl with an assortment of different specialities. Sri Lan-

kans generally order fruit after a meal, finishing with a steaming cup of Ceylon tea.

Breakfast

First thing in the morning, you discover the first great joy of the Sri Lankan table, fresh fruit. The lush tropical climate offers a cornucopia of different varieties. King of them all is the mango, which can be as small as a plum or as large as a king-size coconut. When ripe, the skin can be bright red, purple, pale green or golden, but the flesh inside is always a marvellous yellow with a sweet-sour taste.

To open a mango, stand it on one end and cut it into three vertical sections, running a sharp pointed knife down either side of the flat stone in the centre. Leave the fruit in the skin and make a broad grid of crisscross incisions. When you turn the skin inside out, the fruit will pop up in attractive bite-size cubes.

A rarer delicacy, not to be confused with the mango, is the mangosteen, grown at its best in Kalutara, south of Colombo. At its peak in June, this round purple fruit has bittersweet white segments with a mysterious hint of grape and strawberry. Other tropical delights include the yellow, melon-like papaya, green-skinned guava and golden passion fruit. Popular with Sri Lankans is the exotic durian, delicious despite its nasty smell. Don't be put off by the green skins of the oranges and the drab look of the grapefruit. Sri Lanka hasn't yet succumbed to the wiles of glamourous supermarket presentation; the taste couldn't be finer.

Another local product that you'll enjoy for breakfast is tea. Thanks to the much-maligned British, Ceylon Assam, Orange Pekoe, Flowery Orange Pekoe and Pekoe Souchong flow down from Nuwara Eliya to the table of any decent hotel or restaurant on the island.

Instead of bacon and eggs (though, of course, your hotel will provide this), Sri Lankans begin their day with hoppers. These crisp rice-flour pancakes often have a cooked egg inside. String hoppers, a kind of rice vermicelli, are eaten with a curry of fish or vegetables— for breakfast! Bland rice balls and rice cooked in milk come closer to Western ideas of appropriate breakfast foods.

Curry and its Spices

For a Sri Lankan or Indian cook, the curry powder used in Western countries is an

inferior product, light years removed from their national cuisines. The word "curry" comes from the Tamil *kari*, which means quite simply "sauce". Each authentic curry requires a different combination of spices and ingredients. Following are the basic ones used in every Sri Lankan kitchen. You may want to buy a selection to experiment with back home.

Coriander, ground from a green aromatic leaf or brown

Take your pick of a cornucopia of tropical fruit and eat it on the cool verandah of a colonial hotel.

seed, is basic to the mixture. Turmeric, milled to a powder from small yellow tubers, adds both flavour and colour to rice, fish and meats. Ground ginger root, cumin seeds and red chilli seeds add pungency and fire. In addition, for certain dishes, the flavour is enhanced by sweet cardamon seeds, sticks of cinnamon, nutmeg kernels and cloves.

Coconut milk is a basic ingredient for cooking fish, meat and vegetables, usually in combination with onions or shallots and garlic. Frying is done in very hot coconut oil, which should be well heated before cooking begins so that the sweet coconut flavour disappears. This often makes the difference between a good and a mediocre curry.

The rice is nearly always of the round-grain variety, rather than the long-grained kind favoured by the Indians. It is served either white (plain boiled) or yellow (cooked in coconut milk, with chopped shallots, saffron or turmeric and cinnamon, cloves and cardamom). *Buriyani* rice is cooked in stock and served with hard-boiled eggs and chopped meat, chicken or fish.

The "hotness" of a curry depends on the amount of chilli and ginger added. You can usually judge what's coming by how red the sauce is. If it's on the yellow side, there's an accent on turmeric. Black curry, a speciality of Sri Lanka, takes its colour and rich taste from roasted cumin seeds, the essential ingredient. White curry, without chilli, is the mildest.

Curries are served with floppy breads known as *roti*—made with rice flour, salt, grated coconut and water— and the crisper *poppadoms.* A salad called *sambol* is served either as a first course or as an accompaniment to curried dishes. It combines grated coconut, dried fish, pickles, onions and lemon juice. Grated coconut is always at hand to cool the mouth when eating the hotter curries.

Lamprai, a curried snack **101**

food, consists of rice boiled in bouillon and a dry curry. These are wrapped in a banana leaf and baked.

Seafood

Sri Lanka's marvellous seafood, a speciality of hotels along the south-west coast, stands outside the conflict between "international" and "local" cuisine. Order prawns, squid and spiny lobster (which most menus describe simply as "lobster") curried or grilled. Seafood may also be served with either a mild or spicy sauce topped with grated cheese. Oysters are available in the better hotels and restaurants of Colombo, while Trinco has some excellent crab. The seir-fish, related to mackerel, is disappointing, but there are plenty of other varieties to choose from.

Spiny lobsters are among the best of Sri Lanka's seafood delicacies.

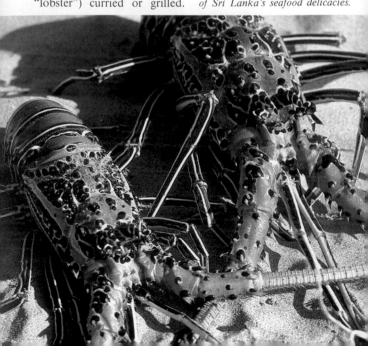

Desserts

After a meal of spicy curries, order cooling curds (from buffalo milk) and treacle. Other local specialities include baked bananas with honey, coconut cake and *wattallapam*, baked caramel custard. Many desserts are based on a combination of rice flour and palm sugar, flavoured with cinnamon, nutmeg and cardamom. *Pani pol* is a sticky little cake of coconut and honey. *Kiri buth* combines rice, coconut and honey. Jaggery is a chewy sweet made from the crystallized sap of the palm tree.

You can also sample recipes handed down from the days of Portuguese and Dutch colonization. Among them are *bolo fiado*, layers of pastry with raisins and cashew nuts, and *fugetti*, candied melon with rosewater.

Drinks

Purists say you should drink nothing cold with your curry, since this will only increase rather than diminish the hotness of the spices. But you can safely sip some water in moderation or, best of all, some beer. The local brands are good. Wine is not recommended, as it spoils the taste of both the curry and the wine. Except in the luxury hotels, it's rarely kept at the right temperature.

Tea is served with more milk and sugar than any but a British-conditioned palate could enjoy. You can also order it black or with lemon. In Sri Lanka, tea is generally better than coffee, which declined in popularity after the crop disaster of the 1870s.

There are two local alcoholic drinks: toddy and arrack. The first is a simple, but often potent, cider-like fermentation of sap from the bud of the coconut flower and the second a powerful distillation of the toddy. In the north, toddy is also made from the palmyrah. Arrack, Sri Lanka's answer to whisky, is available in different strengths and qualities, from "Gal" and "Pol" to "Extra Special" and "Double Distilled". The international hotels serve exotic tropical cocktails based on a variety of fruit juices.

Roadside stands all over the country specialize in Sri Lanka's most popular thirst quencher—coconut water from the *thambili* (king coconut). You just drink the juice through a hole bored in the top of the large orange shell. Fruit juices are also available, but they may not always be safe to drink.

Fish Curry *(Malu Curriya)*

Authentic Sri Lankan curries are not too difficult to prepare if you have the right assortment of spices on hand.

2 lb. of fish
1 medium-sized onion, thinly sliced
2 tsp. salt
2 tsp. chilli powder
2 tsp. coriander
1 tsp. cumin
$\frac{1}{8}$ tsp. turmeric
2-inch piece of cinnamon
2 bay leaves
3 cups coconut milk
1 tbs. lemon juice

Cut the fish into small pieces and wash well. Place in a saucepan with onion, salt, spices and coconut milk. Stir to blend spices. Start cooking over moderate heat and then simmer for 20 minutes. Just before serving, add lemon juice. Serves 4–6.

Fish Balls *(Malu Cutlets)*

This recipe is typical of Sri Lankan home cooking.

1 lb. potatoes
$\frac{1}{2}$ lb. cooked sardines or other fish
$\frac{1}{2}$ lb. chopped onions
2 bay leaves
2 tsp. salt
1 egg white
bread crumbs
oil
butter

Brown the onion in oil. Mash the fish in a small amount of butter. Boil the potatoes and mash with salt, bay leaf and pepper to taste. Combine fish and potatoes, form small balls and dip in egg white. Roll in bread crumbs. Fry in hot oil until golden brown.

BLUEPRINT for a Perfect Trip

How to Get There

Because of the complexity and variability of the many fares available, you should seek the advice of an informed travel agent well before your departure.

N.B. Travel to the Northern and Eastern regions of Sri Lanka should be avoided at the present moment due to separatist violence. Check the current situation with the local authorities before undertaking excursions.

BY AIR

Scheduled Flights

Several scheduled flights depart weekly from London, with one stop-over en route.

Connecting service is available from various North American cities. You may choose to travel due east or west. Schedules vary according to the day of the week.

Charter Flights and Package Tours

While there are no charter flights from Great Britain to Colombo, you can choose from a wide range of package tours, usually lasting for a fortnight. If you don't want to restrict your holiday to Sri Lanka, book a package combining Sri Lanka and Thailand (Bangkok and Pattaya), Sri Lanka and the Maldives, Sri Lanka, Singapore and Penang, or Sri Lanka, Bangkok and Hong Kong, to mention a few examples. Several companies organize flights to Bombay and a tour of southern India, continuing on to Sri Lanka. Indian tour operators also offer extension holidays to Sri Lanka.

To the Maldives

Scheduled service to the Maldives from Colombo is good, and Hulule airport can accommodate all kinds of aircraft, including wide-bodied jets. A direct charter service operates weekly from Frankfurt and Zurich in season.

When to Go

There's nothing monotonous about Sri Lanka's climate. The tropical temperatures of the coastal belt attract sun-worshippers all year round, while the cool dry air of the central hill country provides a brisk change of pace. The best time to visit the island is from October to April, outside the south-west monsoon season (May to September). The north-east monsoon (November to February) usually proves less severe. But even when the monsoon winds blow their hardest, there's sunshine and calm on the opposite side of the island, protected by the central mountain range.

The following chart gives average minimum and maximum temperatures for Colombo, on the coast, and Nuwara Eliya, in the mountains.

		January–April	May–August	September–December
Colombo	°C	23	25	23
	°F	73	77	73
	°C	31	29	29
	°F	88	84	84
Nuwara Eliya	°C	8	12	11
	°F	46	53	52
	°C	21	19	19
	°F	70	66	66

Planning Your Budget

To give you an idea of what to expect, here are a few average prices in Sri Lankan rupees (Rs). They can only be approximate, however, as inflation takes its toll.

Airport. Porter per piece of luggage Rs 5. Taxi to Colombo centre Rs 800, to Negombo Rs 400. Departure tax Rs 400.

Baby-sitters. Rs 60 per hour plus car fare.

Bicycle and motorcycle hire. Bicycles per day Rs 75–100. Motorcycles per day (in advance) Rs 250 (125 cc) to Rs 350 (250 cc), collision damage waiver Rs 100 per day.

Buses. Colombo city bus Rs 5. Ceylon Transport Board coach Colombo to Hikkaduwa Rs 16. Private mini-bus Colombo to Hikkaduwa Rs 18.

Car hire (third-party insurance included). *Datsun Sunny* Rs 550 per day, Rs 5 per km., Rs 5,000 per week with unlimited mileage. *Mitsubishi Colt GLX (AC)* Rs 650 per day, Rs 5 per km., Rs 6,000 per week with unlimited mileage. Collision damage waiver Rs 125 per day. *Chauffeur-driven Peugeot 504* (air-conditioned) Rs 1,320 per day with 800 km. free, additional km. Rs 15 per km., chauffeur subsistence Rs 100 per night out.

Cigarettes. Local brands per packet of 10 Rs 19, imported brands per packet of 20 Rs 65.

Entertainment. Cinema: balcony Rs 21, first class Rs 16, second class Rs 11. Folklore show Rs 250.

Guides. Minimum charge per day Rs 300, plus accommodation and meals on overnight trips.

Hairdressers. *Woman's* cut Rs 165, shampoo and set or blow-dry Rs 330. *Man's* cut Rs 155, shampoo and blow-dry Rs 110.

Hotels (double room with bath per night). *Luxury* Rs 3,000, *moderate* Rs 800. *Guest houses, rest houses* and *inns* Rs 400. *YMCA* single Rs 130, double with bath Rs 250. *YWCA* single Rs 165, double with bath Rs 300.

Meals and drinks. Hotel breakfast Rs 260, lunch Rs 320, dinner Rs 450, lunch or dinner in typical eating houses Rs 250, soft drinks Rs 6 (in hotels Rs 33), beer Rs 48 (in hotels Rs 135), pot of tea Rs 44, king coconut water *(thambili)* Rs 8 (in hotels Rs 33), wine (imported) Rs 700 per bottle.

Taxis and trishaws. Taxis per mile Rs 20, tourist taxis per mile Rs 25, trishaws per mile Rs 15.

An A–Z Summary of Practical Information and Facts

A star (*) following an entry indicates that relevant prices are to be found on page 108.

AIRPORT*. Colombo International Airport (tel.: 030-2911), a modern, air-conditioned complex, lies over 30 kilometres from the city centre at Katunayake. On arrival, you can buy duty-free items at the counter in front of the immigration checkpoint. A taxi, or seats in the airport bus, can be booked at a counter in the arrivals hall. Fares for the 45-minute trip to Colombo are fixed. There are numerous baggage porters, invariably competing for customers. The airport also provides baggage trollies.

The Tourist Information Centre, currency-exchange counter and car-hire desks as well as the post office, police post and restaurant provide 24-hour service. The Sri Lanka Government Railway operates a reservations office during normal business hours.

Airline check-in counters open only shortly before flights take off. Note that the departure tax must be paid in rupees.

For last-minute purchases, stop at the Tea Centre, which sells Ceylon tea specially packaged to carry on board. The duty-free shopping complex in the transit and departure lounge stocks tobacco, perfume, wines, spirits, cameras, watches, gems and precious stones, plus some electrical goods. Payment must be made in foreign currency or traveller's cheques.

BABY-SITTERS. Nearly all hotels can arrange for baby-sitters. Contact the reception desk or housekeeper at least six hours in advance. The cost of transport is added to the basic fee, but there is no surcharge for working after midnight.

BICYCLE and MOTORCYCLE HIRE* (see also DRIVING IN SRI LANKA). Most travel agents can arrange for the hire of a bicycle, and beach hotels usually maintain cycles for the use of their guests. Or you can deal directly with one of the bicycle shops in the beach resorts; just look for the sign "Bicycles for Hire". Make sure that the machine

B is in good working order, particularly brakes and lights. You can bargain over the price, especially for a rental of several days or more. Sri Lanka's humid climate and tropical sun can make cycling a strenuous activity. If possible, avoid the hours between noon and 3 p.m. Remember that road conditions and traffic can be hazardous.

The going will be easier on a motorcycle. Machines ranging from 125 cc. to 250 cc. are available. Most are in reasonable condition, but it's always a good idea to inspect them for possible defects. Hire charges must be paid in advance, plus a refundable deposit of 20% and a small "collison damage waiver". In addition, you'll have to surrender either your passport or air ticket as security. The law requiring helmet to be worn (that has been somewhat ignored in the past) has been reintroduced. It is now illegal for a rider or pillion rider to travel without a helmet. If you really want a helmet, you'll have to insist. You must possess a valid national driving licence.

There are motorcycle hire firms in Colombo and along the southwest coast.

C **CAMPING.** The only official campsite in Sri Lanka is at Sigiriya in the Ancient Cities region. Camping in unauthorized sites is illegal, but the authorities tend to turn a blind eye. However, cheap accommodation is so readily available that camping out just isn't necessary.

CAR HIRE* (see also DRIVING IN SRI LANKA). Not many foreigners dare to drive in Sri Lanka. The hazardous road conditions and freewheeling approach of the locals make a chauffeur-driven car a more sensible choice. What's more, the price is generally less than for self-drive and the chauffeur will act as your guide.

Deal directly with one of the international car-hire firms in Colombo or make arrangements through any travel agent. There are also some local agencies, nearly all of which are reliable. The hire terms are expensive by Asian standards. In the tourist season, advance booking is recommended.

The intrepid few who insist on hiring a self-drive car must be at least 25 years of age, not more than 60 or 65, and hold an international driving licence and valid passport. Most firms accept major credit cards, otherwise a deposit is required.

CIGARETTES, CIGARS, TOBACCO*. Imported tobacco products are expensive in Sri Lanka, but locally made *Gold Leaf*, *Capstan* and **110** *Bristol* cigarettes and pipe tobacco compare favourably with the international brands. Locally made cigars, however, the product of a cottage industry, fall short of their foreign equivalents.

There are no tobacconists as such in Sri Lanka, but cigarettes and tobacco are sold in all small shops. Note that smoking is prohibited in buses, cinemas and theatres.

CLOTHING. Pack for the tropics year-round, unless you plan to visit Sri Lanka's hill country, where the temperature plummets at night. Bring plenty of cool cottons, a hat for protection against the hot noonday sun and sandals or slip-on rubber-soled shoes for sightseeing. Avoid shoes that lace, as you have to remove them when visiting temples.

On the beach, the briefest of swim-wear is acceptable, and although illegal many women go topless at resorts like Hikkaduwa. However it's wise make enquiries before baring all, as the atmosphere of toleration could change and officials may suddenly see fit to enforce the law by prosecuting offenders. When sightseeing in town, avoid immodest attire, especially shorts and low-cut tops.

People may dress up a bit in the evening, particularly in the city. Either a dress or trouser suit would be appropriate for women, and a safari or business suit for men.

COMMUNICATIONS. For relevant opening times, see under HOURS. The General Post Office (G.P.O.) handles stamp sales, parcels, telegrams and domestic telephone service. The main office in Colombo is in Janadhipathi Mawatha, Fort. Letter boxes are painted red and look like their British counterparts. Postal service is generally good, though mail sent from small branches may go astray. Take your letters to the counter and have the stamps cancelled while you watch.

Poste Restante (General Delivery): When picking up mail, you'll have to show your passport or driver's licence. Service is available during general post office hours, as well as about an hour before and after. The Tourist Information Centre also offers poste restante service.

Telegrams: These can be sent from any post office. The Central Telegraph Office, OTS Building, Duke Street, Fort, Colombo, provides round-the-clock service, including Sundays and public holidays. Local telegrams can also be sent over the telephone: dial 133. There are two rates, fast and slow, priced accordingly.

Telephone: Telephoning, even to nearby towns, requires patience. Power failures can and do occur, and lines are often overcharged. Be prepared to wait as long as half an hour. Public call boxes are rare, so you'll have to make calls from hotels or post offices. In Colombo, go to any Overseas Telephone Exchange office. At the Central Overseas Telephone Exchange in the OTS Building operators are on duty 24 hours a day and the telephone directory is in English. Besides the state-owned agencies, telephone, telex, fax and direct-dialling facilities are available at agency post offices in Colombo itself as well as outside.

Outside Colombo, it may be difficult to telephone abroad. Calls are operator-assisted and should be booked in advance.

Telex: Facilities are provided by most of the larger hotels. Or you can send messages via the Central Telex Exchange in the OTS Building, or the nearest branch office.

CONVERTER CHARTS. Only the metric system is used in Sri Lanka. All goods are sold in metres, grams and litres. For fluid and distance measures, see DRIVING IN SRI LANKA.

Weight

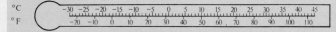

Temperature

Length

CRIME and THEFT. The rapid expansion of tourism has led to a rise in petty crime and theft. It is prudent to take precautions, even in a luxury hotel. Deposit all your valuables (especially cash, cameras, watches, transistor radios and jewellery) in the hotel safe. Any loss or theft should be reported immediately to the nearest police station.

Leave nothing of value on the beach while you swim, and avoid lonely stretches of beach after dusk. In bungalow-style hotel rooms, don't put any of your possessions near an open window, especially at night while you sleep. Beware of pickpockets and purse snatchers in crowded bazaars. Thieves can be very enterprising and tourists are considered fair game.

CUSTOMS and ENTRY REGULATIONS. Nationals of Western Europe and North America who wish to enter Sri Lanka as tourists need only a valid passport for a period of up to one month. However, it is possible to extend the stay on the spot provided you hold a ticket for your onward or return journey and can prove you have sufficient funds for your stay (a minimum per day, variable with inflation).

Department of Immigration and Emigration, Galle Buck Road, Colombo 1; tel.: 29851-5.

In addition, citizens of non-Commonwealth countries must register at Aliens Bureau, 4th Floor, New Secretariat Building, Colombo 1; tel.: 421111

The following chart shows what you may bring into Sri Lanka duty-free, and into your own country when returning home:

Into:	Cigarettes		Cigars		Tobacco	Spirits		Wine
Sri Lanka	200	or	50	or	12 oz.	1½ l. and 2 l.		
Australia	200	or	250 g.	or	250 g.	1 l.	or	1 l.
Canada	200	and	50	and	900 g.	1.1 l.	or	1.1 l.
Eire	200	or	50	or	250 g.	1 l.	and	1 l.
Japan	200	or	50	or	250 g.	3 l.	and	3 l.
N. Zealand	200	or	50	or	250 g.	1.1 l.	and	4.5 l.
U.K.	200	or	50	or	250 g.	1 l.	and	2 l.
U.S.A.	200	and	100	and	*	1 l.	or	1 l.

*a reasonable quantity

113

C **Currency restrictions:** Visitors to Sri Lanka are required to declare the amount of foreign currency in their possession on the official Exchange Control D Form attached to the landing card. You should note all foreign exchange transactions on the form, or keep bank receipts as a record of funds converted into rupees. Only the funds that have been declared on the form can be reconverted into foreign currency when leaving the country. The import or export of local currency is restricted to 250 rupees. It is prohibited to take Indian or Pakistani rupees into the country.

D **DRIVING IN SRI LANKA.** Driving conditions are so difficult that visitors almost always use public transport or hire chauffeur-driven cars. Motorcycles prove somewhat easier to manœuvre, but hire charges are high. There are no expressways or motorways and roads are poorly maintained. Signposting is minimal, and local people seem to regard driving as an exciting, if highly dangerous, sport.

Buses and lorries stop for no one; pedestrians wander in the road, or dart across it without the slightest warning. Stray cattle, cats and dogs are an additional menace—even in the towns. Night driving calls for extra care. Roads are usually very dark and other vehicles, especially bicycles, may not carry lights. When observed, the speed limit in towns and built-up areas is 30 m.p.h., 40 m.p.h. elsewhere. Traffic keeps to the left.

Parking: There are a number of car parks in Colombo. Pay the attendant for the first hour when you leave your car; he'll bill you for the balance when you return. Outside Colombo, you'll have no problem: you either park as required or special car parks exist where fees are levied.

Fuel and oil: Service stations can be found on all main roads and often on major access roads. Only one grade, super (90 octane), is sold, plus diesel fuel and oil.

Fluid measures

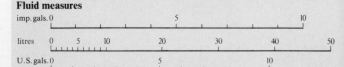

Distance

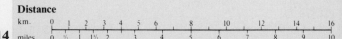

Breakdowns: Call the hire company to rescue you or look for a mechanic to take care of minor problems like flat tires. Breakdowns are such a common occurrence that help will most likely be near at hand. Before you set out, you may want to consult the Automobile Association of Ceylon

40, Sir Macan Markar Mawatha, Galle Face, Colombo 3; tel.: 421528/9, 546074

Accidents: Call the nearest police station and don't move your vehicle until an official report has been made. This is essential for the settlement of any insurance claim.

Traffic Police: See POLICE.

Road distances

Colombo–Mount Lavinia	13 km.
Colombo–Galle	116 km.
Colombo–Trincomalee	257 km.
Colombo–Anuradhapura	206 km.
Colombo–Kandy	116 km.
Colombo–Nuwara Eliya	180 km.
Anuradhapura–Wilpattu	39 km.
Anuradhapura–Polonnaruwa	101 km.
Galle–Mount Lavinia	103 km.

ELECTRIC CURRENT. The standard current is 230–240 volts, 50 cycles A. C. Three-pronged British plugs are used.

EMBASSIES and HIGH COMMISSIONS. Following is a list of foreign missions in Colombo. For additional addresses, consult the local telephone directory or ask at the Travel Information Centre.

Australia: High Commission, 3, Cambridge Place, Colombo 7; tel.: 698767/8/9

Canada: High Commission, 6, Gregory's Road, Colombo 7; tel.: 695841/2/3

U.S.A.: Embassy, 210, Galle Road, Colombo 3; tel.: 448007

Japan: Embassy, 20, Gregory's Road, Colombo 7; tel.: 693831/2/3

United Kingdom: High Commission, 190, Galle Road, Colombo 3; tel.: 437336/7/8/9.

E **EMERGENCIES:** Outside Colombo, call the nearest police station. In the city, dial:

Police	433333	Fire	422222
Ambulance	422222	Hospital	691111

G **GUIDES.** The Ceylon Tourist Board, any travel agent or hotel receptionist can provide you with an English-speaking guide-lecturer. Official guides carry an identity card. Avoid unauthorized guides and touts, however tempting their offers to change your foreign currency or lead you to bargain shops. It is customary to tip guides.

H **HAIRDRESSERS*** (see also TIPPING). The bigger hotels all have good hairdressers and barbers. These shops are accustomed to dealing with foreigners and you'll be well taken care of.

HITCH-HIKING. Although not illegal, hitch-hiking is not recommended. In any case, public transport is so cheap that there's really no need to thumb a ride.

HEALTH and MEDICAL CARE. The prevalence of cholera and, in certain parts of Sri Lanka, malaria pose the most serious health risks. Immunization before departure is, obviously, strongly to be recommended: ask your doctor. You are required to show vaccination certificate for yellow fever only if you arrive within six days after leaving or transiting an infected area. Never drink untreated tap water (see WATER).

Hospitals: Sri Lanka's state hospitals provide free medical and surgical care to tourists and locals alike. But foreigners will receive better care in one of the privately owned and operated hospitals:

Joseph Frazer Memorial Nursing Home, Joseph Frazer Road, Colombo 5; tel.: 588466

Durdan's Hospital, Alfred House, Colombo 3; tel.: 575205/6/7

Nawaloka Hospital, 23 Sri Savgathodaya Mawatha, Colombo 3; tel.: 544444/5/6/7

Asiri Hospitals Ltd, 181 Kirula Road, Colombo 5; tel.: 500608

Chemists: Osu Sala, a state-run pharmacy at Lipton's Circus in **116** Colombo (tel. 694716), is open 24 hours a day. Many other pharmacies remain open till about 10 p.m., including weekends. Imported articles are very expensive, so it's a good idea to bring a sufficient supply of remedies and drug items with you, including sun-tan preparations.

HOTELS and ACCOMMODATION*. Accommodation ranges from the international-style luxury hotels of Colombo and the major beach resorts, most of which have been built in the last five or ten years, to the simple but adequate facilities of the smaller establishments. Generally, even the cheaper hotels are air-conditioned.

Rates for luxury accommodation are invariably quoted in U.S. dollars, rather than in rupees. Tax is included, but a 10% service charge is added to the bill. For details of accommodation in Sri Lanka, enquire at the Travel Information Centre in Colombo.

Any complaints about accommodation should be brought to the attention of the Director of Trade Standards, Ceylon Tourist Board; tel.: 437057.

Guest houses, rest houses and inns are recommended for the budget-conscious. There is no air-conditioning, but most rooms have a fan. Private baths and meals are available. The food is generally wholesome and, if you're lucky, you may enjoy good Sri Lankan home cooking. Neither breakfast nor a service charge of 10% are included in the rate.

Y.M.C.A. and Y.W.C.A. provide basic accommodation in private rooms, as well as nourishing food. These establishments are to be found in Colombo and several other towns. They take the place of youth hostels, of which Sri Lanka has only one—a spartan, dormitory-style lodging in Colombo that is best avoided.

Paying-guest accommodation often equals that of the better guest houses for comfort and cleanliness, though the standard varies considerably. Often widows living in large houses make a few rooms available to visitors. As a rule, the work is done by maids, rather than the owner of the house. A service charge of 10% is usually made.

HOURS

Businesses: 8.30 a.m. to 12.30 p.m. and 1.30–4.30 p.m. Monday to Friday.

Shops: 9 a.m. to 5 or 6 p.m., Monday to Friday; in tourist resorts till 8 or 9 p.m. Half day on Saturdays.

Banks: 9 a.m. to 1 p.m. Monday; 9 a.m. to 1.30 p.m. Tuesday to Friday.

H **Government offices:** 8.30 a.m. to 4.15 p.m. Monday to Friday; although officially open, avoid the hours from 12 to 2 p.m.

Post offices: 8 a.m. to 5 p.m.; Colombo G.P.O., Janadhipathi Mawatha: 24-hour service for stamp sales and local telephone calls only.

Central Overseas Telephone Exchange: 24-hour service, including Sundays and public holidays.

Central Telegraph Office: 24-hour service, including Sundays and public holidays.

Central Telex Exchange: 9 to 2 a.m.

Travel Information Centre: 8.30 a.m. to 4.45 p.m. weekdays; 8.30 a.m. to 12.30 p.m. weekends and holidays.

Fort Railway Station Booking Office: 8.30 a.m. to 3.30 p.m. Monday to Saturday.

Colombo National Museum: 9 a.m. to 5 p.m. Sunday to Thursday; closed Friday and Saturday.

Dehiwela Zoo: 8 a.m. to 6 p.m.

Note: Sri Lankans tend to have a loose notion of time; do not expect absolute punctuality.

L **LANGUAGE** (see also MAPS and PLACE NAMES). There are two national languages—Sinhala, which is spoken by 80 per cent of the people and Tamil. English is the language of trade and commerce. It's widely understood throughout the country, and is the language common to most people in multi-racial Sri Lanka.

Although you'll easily get by with English, one word of Sinhala will stand you in good stead—*āyoubōwan*. Literally "May you live long", it can be used to say everything from "Hello" and "Goodbye" to "Good morning" and "How are you?".

LAUNDRY and DRY-CLEANING. Facilities for both laundry and dry-cleaning are available in most of the larger hotels. Service is usually quick and efficient and cleaning is generally returned within 24 to 48 hours. Local laundries are not recommended for visitors.

LOST PROPERTY. Report losses to your hotel reception desk or the
118 nearest police station.

MAPS and PLACE NAMES. Basic tourist maps are available at the Travel Information Centre. But for more detailed information, try a stationer or contact the Survey Department

Kirula Road, Colombo 5; tel.: 585111/2–5

You'll notice that Sri Lankan place names are a mixed bag of Sinhalese and colonial British: Mahaweli Ganga is the country's longest river, Adam's Peak its sacred mountain. Janadhipathi Mawatha, a Colombo thoroughfare, crosses Chatham Street. Spellings can vary enormously, due to different systems of transcribing Sinhalese script.

Many of the dauntingly long Sinhalese place names, such as Anuradhapura and Pidurutalagala, are actually compound words that incorporate some of the elements below. If you familiarize yourself with these elements, you'll have less of a problem reading area maps and town plans.

arama	monastery, park	**mawatha**	street
deniya	rice field	**para**	road
devale	Buddhist temple	**nuwara**	city
		oya	stream
duwa	island	**pitiya**	park
ela	brook	**pura**	town
gala	rock	**tara, tota**	ford, port
gama	village	**vehara, vihara**	Buddhist temple
ganga	river	**vila**	pond
giri	rock	**wewa**	lake, reservoir
kanda	mountain		

MEETING PEOPLE. The people of Sri Lanka are sociable and easygoing. Communication is never a problem, as English is widely spoken and understood, especially in resort areas. Almost everyone is curious about foreigners. You'll be plied with questions, and perhaps invited home to meet the family of a local acquaintance. But don't be surprised if a few ambitious entrepreneurs turn this friendly contact into an opportunity to make a sale. Sri Lanka is a developing country and many people have to struggle to survive. Beggars may ask you for money, and children for "school pens"; but the wisest course of action is to resist their pleas, as the Tourist Board recommends. Other Sri Lankans will never consider you rude.

M **MONEY MATTERS.** The unit of currency in Sri Lanka is the *rupee* (abbreviated Re or Rs), divided into 100 cents.

Banknotes: Rs 10, 20, 50, 100, 500, 1,000.

Coins: 1, 2, 5, 10, 25, 50 cents; Re 1, Rs 2, 5. (The 1- and 2-cent coins are rarely used.)

For currency restrictions, see CUSTOMS AND ENTRY REGULATIONS.

Banks. Check to see which bank offers the best exchange rate for foreign currency. Don't change too much money at a time, as the reconversion rate is disadvantageous. Remember to take along your passport when cashing traveller's cheques. The Bureau de Change at the Bank of Ceylon is open daily, weekends and holidays included:

York Street, Colombo 1.

Credit cards. Many of the larger hotels and shops accept the well-known international cards.

Prices. Most things are still very reasonable in Sri Lanka, particularly food, clothing, shoes and handicrafts. But bear in mind that many shops charge so-called tourist prices, which may be as much as double what a local resident would pay. Whatever the purchase, bargaining is never out of place—if you go about it in the right spirit. For an idea of the cost of goods and services, see the section PLANNING YOUR BUDGET.

N **NEWSPAPERS and MAGAZINES.** Sri Lanka's English-language dailies include the *Ceylon Daily News,* the *Island* and the *Evening Observer.* The *Sunday Observer, Sunday Times* and the *Island* come out on Sunday. Many hotel bookshops also stock the London dailies, the *International Herald Tribune* and a variety of magazines. They're usually on sale a few days after publication.

P **PHOTOGRAPHY.** Sri Lanka's tropical scenes and year-round sunshine will tempt even the most indifferent of photographers, but be sure to carry sufficient film with you. Both black-and-white and colour film are extremely expensive and local stock is not always fresh. You can have your film processed locally in 24 hours. Note that the X-rays used in airport security checks may harm undeveloped film. To be on the safe side, put film in a bag to be examined separately by the checkers.

Permits are required to photograph the ancient monuments in Anuradhapura, Polonnaruwa and Sigiriya. Apply at the archaeological **120** museums on the various sites. For permits to take photographs at the

Temple of the Tooth in Kandy and the Cave Temple in Dambulla, enquire at the temple offices.

Photographs must be taken in a manner that does not cause disrespect or offend religious susceptibilities. Buddhism is a living religion in Sri Lanka and most ancient monuments are still venerated; posing in front of monuments and paintings is strictly prohibited. Never ask a Buddhist holy man *(bhikku)* to pose for a photo.

POLICE. All towns and townships have police stations open 24 hours a day. Police officers wear khaki uniforms and generally speak English.

The Traffic Police patrols most main roads either on motorcycles or in cars. You'll recognize them by the words "Traffic Police" on their helmets. Another unit, the Tourist Police, is assigned to holiday resorts and the main tourist destinations. In Colombo, Tourist Police Headquarters is situated in the

Police Headquarters, Fort, Colombo 1; tel.: 421111 and ask for "Tourist Police Division".

PUBLIC HOLIDAYS. Business comes to a standstill on public holidays, including monthly Buddhist religious observances when the moon is full. On Full Moon Day *(Poya)*, bars and places of entertainment are closed and no alcohol is served.

January	Thai Pongal (Hindu)
February 4	National Day
February/March	Birthday of the Prophet (Muslim)
	Maha Sivarathri (Hindu)
March/April	Good Friday
April	Sinhalese and Tamil New Year
May	Vesak (Buddhist)
May 1	May Day
May 22	National Heroes' Day
May	Id-Ul-Fitr (end of Ramadan; Muslim)
June 30	Bank Holiday
September/October	Id-Ul-Azha (Haji; Muslim)
	Deepavali (Hindu)
December 25	Christmas Day
December 31	Bank Holiday

R **RADIO and TV.** Radio Sri Lanka broadcasts on two frequencies in Sinhala, Tamil and English. Short-wave programmes of the BBC World Service and Voice of America programmes can also be heard.

Television is transmitted from 4.30 to 11 p.m. daily, plus an hour or two on Sunday mornings. Programmes (in English and the national languages) range from Sinhalese films and locally produced documentaries to BBC offerings, with plenty of commercials in between. TV has become widespread in Sri Lanka, and in luxury hotels you'll find a TV in every room.

RELIGIOUS SERVICES. Sri Lanka is predominantly Buddhist, but there are also many Hindus, Muslims and Christians. Religious freedom is guaranteed under the constitution, but Buddhism has a special status of state protection. The Sri Lankan form of Buddhism, Theravada, is the same as that practised in Burma and Thailand.

Many religious services are conducted in English. Ask at the Travel Information Centre for details of time and place.

T **TABOOS and CUSTOMS.** Sri Lankans take their Buddhist faith seriously. Never try to shake the hand of a Buddhist holy man—or expect him to pose for a photo. Don't cause offence by dressing inappropriately when visiting shrines and temples, and be sure to remove shoes and headcovering before entering. During the once-monthly Buddhist full moon festivals, the sale and public consumption of alcohol is prohibited.

Perhaps the Sri Lankan custom most confusing to foreigners is the practice of indicating "yes" by shaking the head from left to right, and "no" by nodding up and down. Keep this in mind or you may communicate the wrong message.

TIME DIFFERENCES. Sri Lankan time year-round is Greenwich Mean Time plus 5½ hours. The following chart shows winter times in some selected cities. In summer, when British and U.S. clocks advance one hour, Sri Lanka stays the same.

New York	London	**Colombo**	Sydney
1.30 a.m.	6.30 a.m.	**noon**	5.30 p.m.

TIPPING. Keep tips more or less in line with the local standard of living, bearing in mind that 425 or 500 rupees represent a working-man's weekly wage. Hotels, guest houses and restaurants add a service charge to the bill, but it is customary to give something extra to the bell boy, room maid and waiter. See the chart below for further guidelines.

Porter, per bag	Rs 3–5
Hotel maid, per week	Rs 50–60
Bellboy, per errand	Rs 9–10
Waiter	10 % (if service not included)
Taxi or trishaw driver	10 %
Filling station attendant	Rs 5
Hairdresser	10 %

TOILETS. There are no public toilets in Sri Lanka, so you'll have to rely on hotel facilities.

TOURIST INFORMATION. The Ceylon Tourist Board operates the Travel Information Centre
78, Steuart Place, Colombo 3; tel.: 437059/437952/4.

There are branch offices at Colombo International Airport, Port of Colombo and Queen's Hotel (Kandy).

The Centre distributes brochures and maps, as well as information on buses, trains and charter flights. The staff will gladly arrange for guides, suggest itineraries and answer questions about Sri Lankan life and culture. It's wise to make all necessary travel arrangements before leaving Colombo; once you're on the road, information may be hard to come by.

You can have mail sent to you c/o the Tourist Information Centre; there is no charge for the service.

Overseas offices of the Ceylon Tourist Board:

Australia: 439, Albany Highway, Victoria Park, W.A. 6100; tel.: 362-4579

Japan: 2–1, Atago 1 Chome, Minatoku, Tokyo; tel.: 433-6377/8

United Kingdom: London House, 53–54 Haymarket, London SW1Y 4RP; tel.: 321-0034

U.S.A.: Embassy of the Democratic Socialist Republic of Sri Lanka, 2148 Wyoming Ave. N.W., Washington DC 20008; tel.: (202) 483-4025.

TRANSPORT

Buses*: The Ceylon Transport Board, a government company, operates the Colombo city bus system. City buses run from about 5 a.m. to midnight, but service is irregular in the early hours of the morning and after 10 p.m. This is not a practical way to get around, as buses are always extremely overcrowded and slow, whatever the time of day.

Taxi*: There is taxi service in Colombo and the larger towns and the taxis always display the word "Taxi". Elsewhere, taxis are indistinguishable from normal vehicles, but this is never a problem; drivers always rush up to any likely-looking foreigner with a searching look. Most drivers speak English. Taxis are generally equipped with meters, but drivers often fail to use them. Be sure to ask the driver to turn on the meter; if it's out of order, agree on the fare in advance. Ace Radio Cab (tel.: 501502/3/4) and Kangaroo Cabs (tel.: 502888) offer radio controlled cabs from a central point and offer customers a standard rate per kilometre with a minimum charge and waiting charges.

Trishaws*: These slow-moving three-wheeled pedicabs can be fun for short trips. Trishaws carry two passengers and cost less than taxis. Best negotiate the price before you set out.

Long-distance mini-buses*: Although the Ceylon Transport Board maintains an extensive network of coaches, the parallel service offered by competing private operators is far more efficient and still very cheap. Buses leave from the Fort Railway Station in Colombo as soon as a full load of passengers is on board. There are neither route maps nor timetables. If you want to travel to a distant town, be sure to arrive at the station as early as possible in the day. For nearby destinations, buses depart at regular intervals. You never have to wait very long.

Trains*: Ceylon Government Railway (CGR) trains run to all the popular tourist spots in Sri Lanka, but don't expect to arrive at your destination quickly. For example, service from Colombo to Trinco-malee, a distance of some 250 kilometres, takes well over six hours.

There are some first-class air-conditioned cars, sleeping berths and "observation saloons". Otherwise, you have a choice of spartan second and third, where seats are wooden benches. Third-class passengers pile into what appear to be cattle cars; windows are high, narrow and open to the air. You can, at least, enjoy the view in second; windows are bigger and may be fitted with glass, depending on whether or not it's been broken. All trains have toilet facilities, some have restaurant cars. Seats can be reserved in advance. For bookings contact:

Railtours, Fort Railway Station, Colombo 1; tel.: 435838 or the Fort Railway Station, Colombo; tel.: 421281, ext. 389.

The CGR offers all-inclusive day tours by first-class train to Kandy, Hikkaduwa and Polonnaruwa. For reservations, enquire at your hotel reception desk or the Tourist Office in the Fort Railway Station (tel.: 35838).

Internal Flights: Upali Aviation operates a limited scheduled heli-copter and light aircraft service. For information get in touch with the firm:

34, Galle Rd, Galle Face, Colombo 3; tel.: 20465/28826/29399.

WATER. Don't drink the tap water in Sri Lanka, unless it has been boiled and filtered. Most of the bigger hotels have treated water. Else-where stick to the bottled variety. A good thirst quencher available everywhere is the water of the king coconut *(thambili)* drunk straight from the shell.

Index

An asterisk (*) next to a page number indicates a map reference. For index to Practical Information, see inside front cover.

099/110 SUD 27